GW00361282

HENK VAN OORT, born in 1943,
school teacher before taking a Maste
the Amsterdam University. He has
primary and secondary education, including within the
Steiner school system and adult educational courses and
seminars for teachers and parents. His interest in literature
has led him to teach at storytelling and poetry seminars. He
leads hugely popular introductory courses to anthroposophy,
and is the author of *Anthroposophy, A Concise Introduction to
Rudolf Steiner's Philosophy*. Based in Bergen N.H. in the
Netherlands, Henk van Oort is married and the father of
three grown-up children.

Anthroposophy A–Z

A Glossary of Terms Relating to
Rudolf Steiner's Spiritual Philosophy

Henk van Oort

Sophia Books

Sophia Books
Hillside House, The Square
Forest Row, East Sussex RH18 5ES

www.rudolfsteinerpress.com

Published by Sophia Books 2011
An imprint of Rudolf Steiner Press

Originally published in Dutch under the title *Lexicon antroposofie* in 2010
by Uitgeverij Christofoor, Zeist. Translated from Dutch by the author, and
edited by Rudolf Steiner Press

A catalogue record for this book is available from the British Library

ISBN 978 1 85584 264 9

Cover by Andrew Morgan Design
Typeset by DP Photosetting, Neath, West Glamorgan
Printed and bound by Gutenberg Press, Malta

MIX
Paper from
responsible sources
FSC® C022612

Foreword

This glossary is intended as a helpful reference volume for those who take an interest in Rudolf Steiner's anthroposophy, or wish to find out more about it. The main anthroposophic terms are discussed and defined, or explained. With an eye to the wide range of potential readers, I have included basic terms as well as less frequently used ones. However, I have not tried to provide an exhaustive compendium. Anthroposophy sheds light on so many fields that this would scarcely be possible. To enhance understanding, it may be a good idea to look up more than one term, and for this purpose I have provided asterisks to indicate related search terms in this volume.

The glossary is the result of hands-on experience of teaching anthroposophy to parents and teachers at Waldorf schools, and to course participants in other anthroposophic fields of work. A good understanding of typical anthroposophic terms is very helpful for delving further into Rudolf Steiner's spiritual science. Defining terms and concepts is a crucial part of my courses; only after acquiring a clear picture of what is meant will course participants be able to use the new terminology as a tool for personal enquiry and self-development.

In my conversations with people of quite different persuasions, it has become evident that a clear outline of the terms I use is necessary to prevent huge, Babel-like confusion. From my experience with international audiences in many countries, all speaking different languages, I know that every word has to be carefully weighed before it can convey the intended message. However difficult this may be, as long as we are aware of the potential linguistic pitfalls we can hone our concepts so that others really understand us, and we in turn understand them.

Anthroposophy is also a language, one that can connect us with the reality of the spiritual world. This is why I embarked on writing an anthroposophic glossary in English, which I hope will reach a worldwide readership. As I began to compile it, I realized that it would have been very helpful to me 40 years ago, when I first encountered anthroposophy.

Henk van Oort
June 2011

Note: An asterisk before a word indicates that a full entry can be found in the Glossary.

A

Advent — the period of four weeks leading up to [*]Christmas, marked especially by the first, second, third and fourth Sundays. Ample attention is paid to this period in [*]Waldorf schools. On the Monday morning after each Advent Sunday, pupils gather in the school hall to sing Advent songs about the forthcoming birth of [*]Jesus. Each week, one more candle is lit on the Advent wreath made of fir branches. When all four candles on the wreath are burning, everyone knows that Christmas will come in the next few days.

In nursery schools, an Advent spiral of fir branches is laid out on the floor. Accompanied by lyre music, each child in turn walks through this spiral and lights a candle from the big candle at the centre of the spiral. The burning candles are placed in the spiral thus creating a beautiful, luminous spiral on the floor.

If a crib scene is on display at home or in class, the following custom is often observed: small stones are placed in and around the stable on the first Advent Sunday. On the second Advent Sunday some plants are added. On the third Advent, toy animals appear near or in the stable. On the fourth Advent, human figures — Joseph and Mary — follow. On Christmas Day, the Jesus child is laid in the manger. The whole sequence represents an evolution towards the arrival of the highest possible human potential — the human being's higher [*]'I' — with which Christ can unite through his own descent to earth.

Rudolf Steiner: *The Festivals and Their Meaning*.

---

[*] GA = *Gesamtausgabe*, referring to the Collected Works of Rudolf Steiner. See page 135 for a full list of titles referred to.

Ahriman

Ahriman — a divine being whose name originates in the Ancient Persian *cultural period, and the opponent of *Ahura Mazda, the Persian sun god. According to Rudolf *Steiner the influence of Ahriman is still very much present. Ahriman is the chief cause of all processes that harden and materialize what were initially spiritual realities underlying all Creation. These hardening processes are essential to life on *earth. For instance, originating from a spiritual archetype, the human skeleton develops from a liquid substance through a stage of cartilage into a rigid skeleton, which enables us to stand upright and resist gravity. This process took place during the earth's evolutionary stages and is repeated in the developmental stages of the human and animal foetus (see: Biogenetic law). Ahriman tries to harden all substances, even in places where these substances should remain supple or fluid. Frozen concepts and fossilized traditions, but also hardened blood vessels, are the results of Ahriman's dominating influence in the wrong places. Ahriman is essential to all life on earth but must continually be kept in his rightful place, for otherwise he causes great harm. The essential balance between Ahriman on the one hand, and *Lucifer on the other, is held by Christ, as depicted by Rudolf *Steiner in his wooden sculpture 'The *Representative of Humanity', now housed at the *Goetheanum in Dornach, Switzerland.

Rudolf Steiner: *The Tension Between East and West*, GA 83*.

Ahura Mazda — a divine being of the Ancient Persian *cultural period. Traditionally located in the sun, he is often depicted as the sun disc with wings. His opponent is *Ahriman. *Zarathustra (= Zoroaster) was ordered by Ahura Mazda to teach people how to cultivate the soil and how to domesticate animals — things that had never been done before. For instance, wild grass was gradually transformed into grain, and wild roses were eventually turned into edible apples. Ahura Mazda is one of the many names of the deity who is associated with the sun. Successive civilizations have always recognized this divine being, giving it various names. In *anthroposophy this historical sequence eventually leads up to the manifestation of *Christ.

Rudolf Steiner: *The Tension Between East and West*, GA 83.

Akasha Chronicle — a chronicle or record that is imperceptible to the ordinary senses, into which are inscribed all events that occur in the cosmos and the history of humanity. Thus it is a 'cosmic memory' of all that happens. Nothing is forgotten. The *initiate can 'read' this chronicle and thus reveal events that have long been forgotten. Not only events that took place in the physical world can be unveiled, but also underlying spiritual connections. Rudolf *Steiner developed the capacity to read this supersensible chronicle.

Rudolf Steiner: *Cosmic Memory*, GA 11.

Alcohol — drinking alcohol causes the astral body to loosen itself from the *physical and *etheric bodies. Awareness of the physical body diminishes, causing a pleasant and relaxing sensation. However, after a couple of hours, when the alcohol has worn off, the astral body will dive back into the etheric and physical body with considerable force. It does this in such a way that the attachment between the four *members becomes more intense. By drinking alcohol on a regular basis, the four members eventually become more firmly interconnected than before, and engage in processes that are mainly focused on the physical world. This excessive attachment between the four members is the cause of pain during a hangover or, worse, the state of alcoholism. Alcohol takes command and thus prevents a person's *'I' from acting fully. From an historical point of view, this general effect was precisely the mission of alcohol. In Ancient Greece, *Dionysus was worshipped as the god who gave alcohol and all its pleasures to mankind. At that stage of human evolution, people had to learn to focus on earthly matters, and alcohol was a tool to do so.

Rudolf Steiner: *From Comets to Cocaine*, GA 348.

Angel — spiritual being nearest to the human being, belonging to the third *hierarchy. The general task of angels is to guide us through life. Angels focus their guiding activities on enabling us to experience the spiritual world through the power of *imaginative thought. They do this by instilling spiritual images into the *astral body when people are asleep. Through the *consciousness soul we can become more aware of this process, discovering that the physical world has arisen from spiritual concepts and realities.

Rudolf Steiner: *Spiritual Hierarchies and the Physical World*, GA 110; *The Work of the Angel in Our Astral Body*, GA 182.

Animal — see: Mankind

Anthroposophical Leading Thoughts — Compilation of concepts and ideas that form the basis of anthroposophy, formulated by Rudolf *Steiner between February 1924 and April 1925. Although this compilation is meant for students of *anthroposophy, it is also intended as stimulus for those who wish to develop and spread anthroposophy in an active way. Discussions in study groups can be centred on these thoughts, which can be regarded as a modern path of knowledge. Rudolf Steiner used these texts to try to help shape the Anthroposophical Society as a place where anthroposophy can be preserved and safeguarded.

Rudolf Steiner: *Anthroposophical Leading Thoughts*, GA 26.

Anthroposophical Society — founded in Germany in 1912 around Rudolf *Steiner, who until then had been chairman of the German branch of the Theosophical Society for ten years. The founding of the Anthroposophical Society marked a split from the theosophists (see: Theosophy). Rudolf Steiner did not initially assume any official function in the Anthroposophical Society, doing so only in 1923, when he became its president until his death in 1925. The main aim of the Anthroposophical Society is to develop and disseminate Rudolf Steiner's spiritual science and demonstrate how this can be fruitful in addressing the needs of the contemporary world. There are branches of the Anthroposophical Society throughout the world. The headquarters of this society, whose full name is the 'General Anthroposophical Society', are located in *Dornach, Switzerland.

Rudolf Steiner: *Anthroposophical Leading Thoughts*, GA 26.

Anthroposophy — the word means, wisdom and knowledge of the human being. The term was first used by Robert Zimmermann, teacher at the Technical High School in Vienna, Austria, where Rudolf *Steiner was a student in 1879. The Greek word 'anthropos' literally means 'the one who looks up'. Unlike animals, human beings can consciously look up at the sky and thus try to establish contact with the stars and other celestial bodies, and the invisible beings who dwell in them. When Rudolf Steiner left the Theosophical Society in 1913 he decided to use the term 'anthroposophy' for his modern spiritual science.

Henk van Oort: *Anthroposophy, a Concise Introduction to Rudolf Steiner's Spiritual Philosophy*.

Antipathy — By developing antipathy in the broadest sense of the world, we are able to create distance between ourselves and the surrounding world. This faculty for developing antipathy is located in the nervous system, and particularly in the *senses. By means of the nervous system and the senses we become aware of our surroundings. Without antipathy, we would remain entirely given up to sense impressions in a dream-like state such as we find in very young children. Initially they are full of *sympathy, and part and parcel of their surroundings. In growing up they gradually develop antipathy and thus grow more aware of the surrounding world. In the sequence *thinking, *feeling and *will, antipathy can be found in its clearest form in thinking. See also: Sympathy.

Rudolf Steiner: *Study of Man*, GA 293.

Apollonian — adjective belonging to Apollo, the Greek god of music and poetry. In *anthroposophy, this is used to refer to the formative forces emanating from the power of thought located in the head. Concepts such as 'order', 'rest', 'cool' and 'motionless' define the scope of this field of energy.

It is sometimes said that one should keep one's head cool to make the right decisions. A hothead cannot assess a dangerous situation. The opposite of Apollonian is *Dionysian, in this context referring to the forces arising in digestive organs and the *will. In *Waldorf education, teachers try to organize their lessons in such a way that Apollonian and Dionysian activities alternate to create a balanced and living dynamic.

Rudolf Steiner: *Practical Advice to Teachers*, GA 294.

Archai — spiritual beings belonging to the third *hierarchy. Also called 'Spirits of Personality' or 'Epoch Spirits'. During the *reincarnation process these spirits accomplish the differentiation of the human *'I' as the basis for what is called 'personality'. The archai work to engender a future type of human being who can be entirely self-directing and independent. They see to it that human beings are born at a particular moment and in a particular place so that they will be able to meet other human beings on *earth in correspondence with and fulfilment of their *karma.

Rudolf Steiner: *Spiritual Hierarchies and the Physical World*, GA 110.

Archangel — spiritual being belonging to the third *hierarchy.

An archangel can serve as a national spirit, inspiring a whole nation with all its characteristics such as language, ethics and folk customs. Expressions such as 'folk-soul' and 'folk-spirit' indicate the same spiritual being. Of the many archangels, Rudolf *Steiner mentions seven in particular who alternate as serving Epoch Spirits. These seven archangels are: Oriphiel (200 BC–150 AD), Anael (150–500), Zachariel (500–850), Raphael (850–1190), Samael (1190–1510), Gabriel (1510–1879), *Michael (1879–2300). This sequence should be understood as a repeating cycle.

Rudolf Steiner: *The Cycle of the Year*, GA 223; *The Festivals and their Meaning*.

Architecture — see: Organic architecture.

Arthurian stream — one of the four *mystery streams that form the basis of *anthroposophy. This mystery stream originates, from a European point of view, in the West, and is linked to Hibernia (= Ireland), Celtic Christianity and the legendary figure of King Arthur. Stone circles such as Stonehenge in the south of England gave the name Megalithic culture to this spiritual impulse. The Druids were their priests. In the etheric aura of the *earth, they witnessed *Christ approaching our planet. The Druids called Christ the 'Lord of the *Elements'. The legends of St Bride relate to this. The monk Columba took Celtic Christianity from Ireland via the isle of Iona to England where, in the seventh century AD, it disappeared from the visible world. However, it remained active in the spiritual world and resurfaced again in anthroposophy.

B.C. Lievegoed: *Mystery Streams in Europe and the New Mysteries*.

Astral body — one of the four members or 'bodies' of the human being. Animals also have an astral body. Awareness and self-awareness including all feelings and intentions are located in the astral body.

The astral body also enables us to move. This aspect of

the astral body can be compared with the strings of a puppet. The puppeteer can be compared with the *'I' that governs all movements. The astral body is born from closer involvement in the physical and etheric bodies to a state of relative independence at about the age of 14, at sexual maturity.

The astral body is related to the *element of air. While breathing in, the astral body is drawn into the *physical body. While breathing out, the link between the astral and the physical bodies is loosened again.

The astral body also expresses itself in colours, which may be regarded as a manifestation of the astral world in the physical world. The *plant, not having an astral body, just touches into the astral world, so to speak, in the colourful flower. And the mood present in our astral body early in the morning, when we dress, may often determine what colours we wear that day.

The feelings and intentions in our astral body can be so strong that the 'I' cannot master them anymore. This dangerous situation may be compared to a zoo with cages but no bars. The astral body takes over and can be harmful and destructive in such a situation. When we sleep the 'I' and the astral body leave the *ether body and the physical body, which stay in bed. The 'I' and the astral body remain in the spiritual world during sleep and re-enter the ether body and the physical body when waking up. After death the ether body, the astral body and the 'I' leave the physical body, which starts to disintegrate. After death the astral body stays with the 'I' for a period of about one third of the life that has just come to an end. This period is called *kamaloka. After this the astral body dissolves in the general astral world of the cosmos.

Rudolf Steiner: *Theosophy*, GA 9; *The Education of the Child*, GA 34.

Asuras — retarded spiritual beings belonging to the *hierarchy of the *archai. There are higher and lower asuras, both involved in the development of the human *'I'. The higher asuras play a positive role in this process. The lower asuras are the spirits of temptation who penetrate and exacerbate the impulses of *Ahriman and *Lucifer. By penetrating the human *consciousness soul, the lower asuras try to lure us into the belief that the physical world is the only reality. Awareness of any spiritual element gets blocked. In this way human beings come to believe that they are just higher animals that have evolved from the animal kingdom.

Rudolf Steiner: *The Deed of Christ*, GA 107.

Atavistic — in anthroposophy often combined with the concept of *clairvoyance. Atavistic clairvoyance means that someone is clairvoyant to a certain degree but cannot direct and control this faculty with the *'I'. This type of clairvoyance stems from a preceding stage of human evolution when clairvoyance ungoverned by the 'I' was the norm. *Anthroposophy aims at a new kind of consciously developed and controlled clairvoyance in which the 'I' has full control of the whole process.

Rudolf Steiner: *Theosophy*, GA 9.

Atlantis — a submerged continent, located where we now find the Atlantic Ocean. It was swallowed up by an enormous tsunami around 10,000 BC. Before this disaster, *Manu led a group of people away from Atlantis. He took them to present-day India, where the Ancient Indian *cultural period started. Rudolf *Steiner describes the Atlantean culture in many texts and lectures. Plato mentions Atlantis in his dialogue *Critias*. Rudolf Steiner's information about Atlantis puts the various developmental stages, of humanity into an entirely new perspective. New light is shed on our evolutionary stages from Ancient *Saturn to the present day. The gulf stream in the Atlantic Ocean

roughly indicates the outline of this sunken continent. See
also: Planetary stages.

Rudolf Steiner: *Cosmic Memory*, GA 11.

Atma — see: Spirit Man.

Aura — a non-material colourful energy field in and around
*minerals, *plants, *animals and *human beings. It can only
be perceived by those who have developed a certain degree
of *clairvoyance. In the aura, with its continually moving
and changing range of colours, a clairvoyant can see qualities and characteristics that remain hidden to the physical
eye. Both perception and interpretation of this phenomenon are strongly dependent on the level of clairvoyance of
the observer. For this reason aura reading should be done
with extreme care.

Rudolf Steiner: *Theosophy*, GA 9.

B

Balance, sense of — one of the 12 *senses. Through this sense we create a personal space around our physical body in which we can be fully awake. Within this space we are clearly aware of spatial orientation: in front/ behind, above/below and left/right. With the help of this sense we determine, both literally and figuratively, our own standpoint, within which the *'I' can perform its daily tasks. In order to under*stand* somebody one must be able to *stand* in balance.

Rudolf Steiner: *Study of Man*, GA 293; Albert Soesman: *Our Twelve Senses*.

Biodynamic — a method of organic farming (agriculture, dairy, horticulture) based on suggestions which Rudolf *Steiner gave during the Agriculture Course in Koberwitz, now Poland, in 1924. An emphasis is placed on the 'whole organism' of crops, livestock and the people who live on the farm. In the course, a comprehensive picture is given of the dynamic relationships in nature. Influences of cosmic constellations and of spiritual entities are taken into consideration. Fields and compost heaps are treated with special *'preparations' in order to enliven and protect natural processes. 'Biodynamic' is a trademark held by the 'Demeter' organization, which has become known throughout the world. See: Zodiac.

Rudolf Steiner: *Agriculture Course*, GA 327.

Biogenetic Law — formulated by the German philosopher Ernst Haeckel (1834–1919): *Ontogeny recapitulates phylogeny*. In other words, human development from embryonic cell to adulthood is a condensed repetition of the sequence that our ancestors passed through from originating

13

Creation in the distant past until now. It is also called the 'theory of recapitulation'.

Rudolf *Steiner endorsed this point of view and used the concept when he drew up the curriculum of the first *Waldorf school. During consecutive school years the student passes through the various stages of consciousness that humanity underwent in its previous evolution, experiencing such stages, for instance, in stories and study material from the successive cultures of ancient India, Persia, Egypt, Greece and Rome.

Rudolf Steiner: *Study of Man*, GA 293.

Biography — description of someone's life by another i.e. 'external' author. The internal author of our life, however, is our higher *'I'. In the external description of someone's life we learn, in a more or less chronological order, how their life unfolded. In an anthroposophically inspired biography we come to know the most obvious elements of a life but also the seemingly unimportant but nevertheless decisive elements. All these elements are linked to *karma. Since the higher 'I', the author of biography, travels from life to life through *reincarnation, all elements must be seen in the light of this. Knowledge of this process can shed clarifying light on the events in one's own life.

Rudolf Steiner: *Manifestations of Karma*, GA 120; *Reincarnation and Karma*, GA 135.

Block teaching — in *Waldorf teaching the main subjects such as reading, writing, arithmetic, history or geography are taught during the first two hours of the day, usually for a period of three to four consecutive weeks. This block teaching is one distinguishing feature of Waldorf teaching. In the intermediate time between two blocks covering the same theme or area, the subject matter has a chance to really sink in. There are no distracting influences of other subjects during such a period, so the focus is thorough and intense.

At a subconscious level the subject matter is thoroughly digested, permeating the four human *members or bodies, and is therefore subsequently available to a pupil in a more profound and lasting way (see: Sleep). On a regular school day, the first two-hour block is usually followed by other subjects lessons lasting one hour, such as foreign languages, music, handicraft, physical education, etc.

Rudolf Steiner: *Practical Advice to Teachers*, GA 294.

Blood — carrier of the *'I'. Antipole of the *nerves. Blood has a tendency to 'evaporate' into *spirit. The nerve has a tendency to harden into bone, into *skeleton. These two poles are respectively centred in the metabolic system (abdomen and limbs where, relatively, much blood is present) and in the head (nerves and senses, where blood is less present). Blood enables us to take in the surrounding world with *sympathy. The nerves enable us to consciously oppose the surrounding world with *antipathy. The mediating rhythmic activity of heart and lungs keeps the two opposing poles in balance. The clear distinction between nerves and blood plays an important part in the anthroposophic concept of the human being as the basis of all anthroposophic *fields of work.

Rudolf Steiner: *Study of Man*, GA 293.

Bodhisattva — an *initiate, or enlightened being, who acts as a teacher of mankind for a certain period. When that period has elapsed, the bodhisattva attains the rank of buddha and will not incarnate again in a physical body on *earth.

Rudolf Steiner: *The Reappearance of Christ*, GA 118; *From Buddha to Christ*, GA 58.

Bodily sheaths — see: Members.

Body — in a general sense referring to earthly matter originating from a spiritual source, and often cited in the context of *body,*soul,*spirit. The human body is usually referred to as *'physical body'. *Anthroposophy tells us

15

that rather than *being* a body we *have* a body inhabited by the *'I'.

Rudolf Steiner: *Theosophy*, GA 9.

Brain — the brain acts as a mirroring ground upon which *thinking can manifest. By so doing it mediates between the spiritual and the physical world just as a radio mediates between the broadcaster and the listener. Most radio stations are broadcasting their programmes 24 hours a day; but the only station we can hear is the one we tune in to. In the same way, the *'I' chooses from available possibilities and limitations the thoughts that are relevant at a particular moment. The brain does not produce thoughts. It raises the thinking activity of the mind into consciousness. The term 'mindsight' refers to this reflective ability of the brain. Recent brain research has shown that *will and manual activity, and the 'I' with its choice of thoughts, exert influence on the physical structure of the brain, especially in young children. Not only do hereditary properties shape the brain, but actions and thoughts also do. This process goes on throughout life. See also: Thinking, Waldorf education.

Rudolf Steiner: *Study of Man*, GA 293; Pim van Lommel: *Endless Consciousness*; Daniel Siegel: *Mindsight*.

Buddha — not a proper name but a rank. When buddha-status is reached by a *bodhisattva, no further *incarnations in a *physical body on *earth are necessary. The buddha is then able to guide mankind from the spiritual world. After Siddhartha Gautama reached buddha-status in the fourth century before Christ it will, according to Rudolf *Steiner, take 5000 years until the next bodhisattva is elevated to this level. This will be the Maitreya Buddha. Until that time the bodhisattva will work in each century as a high *initiate to guide mankind on its further development.

Rudolf Steiner: *The Gospel of St Luke*, GA 114.

C

Calendar of the Soul — Rudolf *Steiner gave 52 verses, each one relating to a week of the year. This calendar enables the human *soul to participate in the year's seasonal changes. The sequence starts in the week after *Easter, which is seen as the first week of the year: thus not the birth of *Jesus but the birth of *Christ is regarded as the start of a process of annual renewal. The weekly verses are meant to awaken and strengthen the soul so that the human *'I', which itself mirrors Christ, can manifest. Only after Christ's incarnation and resurrection was it possible for the human being to really develop his own 'I' consciousness. These verses accompany the human *soul through the year from Christ's birth on *earth to Christ's birth in all *mankind.

Rudolf Steiner: *The Calendar of the Soul*, GA 40; H.D. van Goudoever: *A Contemplation about Rudolf Steiner's Calendar of the Soul*.

Camphill movement — see: Social therapy.

Celtic Christianity — see: Mystery streams.

Certificates — at the end of each school year, students in *Waldorf schools are given a certificate along with a report on the past year's achievements. A personalized verse or maxim is an essential part of the certificate. The teacher usually draws inspiration for this from the subject matter studied during that year. In this verse the student is offered an image in which he will recognize himself, or will feel supported. Very often the pupil speaks the verse aloud in front of the class one morning a week during the following year, for a certain period of time. Not only the content of the verse, but also the rhythm in which it is written, has a pedagogical effect. Even the quality of the sounds that appear as vowels and consonants is taken into considera-

17

tion when the teacher writes these very personalized verses. At the end of the years of schooling at a Waldorf school, a student receives a Waldorf certificate, above and beyond exam certificates, in which all additional subjects and activities are mentioned. To achieve greater uniformity between Waldorf certificates in Europe, the European Council for Steiner Waldorf Education (ECSWE) has created a European Portfolio Certificate (EPC) for students who have completed a Steiner Waldorf School education. The ECSWE, backed by the European Council and representing 650 Waldorf schools in Europe, is seeking recognition of this portfolio from vocational and academic institutions.

Rudolf Steiner: *Discussions with Teachers, GA 295; Spiritual Ground of Education*, GA 305.

Chakra — organ in the *ether body and in the *astral body, also called lotus flower. A chakra mediates between the spiritual and the physical world. From tail bone to the top of the head the main chakras are: root chakra, sacral chakra, navel chakra, heart chakra, throat chakra, brow chakra, crown chakra. When a chakra is open, in movement, it is active and can do its work. Chakras also act as organs of perception of events not perceived by the physical *senses. In this way the chakras help determine our psychological make-up. Due to the fact that the human *members have been 'telescoped' into one another over the ages, the chakras became less active. Their ability to do their work was hampered by a certain degree of fossilization. However, the time has come when the human bodily sheaths or members will be loosened from each other again, resulting in reactivation of the chakras. A new form of *clairvoyance is gradually arising, though now with a personal, *I-sustained consciousness. Rudolf *Steiner mentions the seven main chakras in his books and lectures. The anthroposophical esoteric soul exercises lead to activation of the chakras and to further development of the soul faculties of *imagination, *inspiration and *intuition.

Rudolf Steiner: *Esoteric Lessons*, GA 266; *Knowledge of the Higher Worlds*, GA 10; Anodea Judith: *Eastern Body, Western Mind.*

Change of teeth — the *physical body is born at the start of life on *earth. Around the age of seven, the *ether body is born, becoming free from growth and life processes and more available for mental faculties such as memory and school learning. Around 14, the *astral body is born, so that an independent life of individual feeling develops; and around 21 the *'I' is born, accompanied by increasing awareness of our goals and mission in life. Thus we experience four births on our path to adulthood. The birth of the ether body is a sign that primary growth processes have been completed, and that the child has made the body he inherited at birth into his own. The milk teeth are pushed out by the second teeth, as a visible demonstration of this emancipation of the ether body. If learning processes with an intellectual character begin before the ether forces are released from primary growth processes, the development of the physical body can be hampered. Though the age of second dentition varies between cultures and races, the phenomenon invariably indicates the process described above.

Rudolf Steiner: *The Education of the Child*, GA 34.

Chartres — town in France, south west of Paris. In the twelfth century, this was an important Christian neo-Platonic centre of learning, with famous scholars such as Alanus ab Insulis and Brunetto Latini. The latter was Dante's teacher. In Dante's *Divine Comedy* some influence of the school of Chartres can be found. Rudolf *Steiner reveals that, after their deaths, these Platonic scholars met the followers of Aristotle in the spiritual world. After this meeting these followers of Aristotle reincarnated as Dominican monks. In the fifteenth century both groups, the Platonic and the Aristotelian scholars, were in the spiritual world. It was there that the esoteric School of *Michael was founded. Raphael's painting of the 'School of Athens' may have been inspired by this esoteric event. In *anthroposophy, both schools of thought, Platonic and Aristotelian, are represented.

René Querido: *The Golden Age of Chartres;* Rudolf Steiner: *Karmic Relationships Vol. 6*, GA 240.

Cherubim — spiritual beings belonging to the first *hierarchy. Also called 'Spirits of Harmony'. They transformed the ideas of the *Seraphim, the basis for creating our solar system, into actual configurations forming the human being and his world.

Rudolf Steiner: *The Spiritual Beings and the Physical World*, GA 110.

Childhood diseases — these specific diseases result from a necessary developmental process in which a human being tries to overcome influences from the inherited *physical body. The child must bring inherited substances into line with his own *'I', a process that culminates in the *change of teeth. The intensity of this process depends on the degree of conformity between the physical body and the 'I'. The bigger the difference, the more intense the harmonization process expressed in these types of disease will have to be. This basic concept of the origin of childhood diseases has been complicated by new forms of medication that suppress symptoms (vaccination). Although these medicines are widely applied to prevent childhood diseases, it is clear that the harmonization process is partly blocked by their use.

Rudolf Steiner: *Introducing Anthroposophical Medicine*, GA 312.

Children's games — many traditional children's games originate from long-standing traditions. Ring games, where one child passes around the circle, for example, represent a protective space reminiscent of the period before birth, during which they had to 'wander' in search of their next *incarnation. The texts of these games can be understood at various levels. Awareness of their deeper significance can shed inspiring light on seemingly simple rhymes and can become an incentive to educators to play these games with the children in their care. These traditional games support children in the process of growing up.

Iona and Peter Opie: *Children's Games in Street and Playground.*

Chladni figures — Ernst Chladni (1756–1827) designed a method to show how sound configures matter by producing all sorts of figures in loose sand on a flat plate. When a violin bow is drawn along the edge of the plate, parts of the plate will start to vibrate while other parts remain still. Where the plate vibrates, the sand jumps and rolls to a still part. The pitch of the tone will cause a corresponding figure. There are as many figures as there are tones. Rudolf *Steiner mentions these Chladni figures when he speaks about the *Harmony of the Spheres and the *sound ether.

Rudolf Steiner: *Anthroposophical Spiritual Science and Medical Therapy*, GA 313; *Foundations of Esotericism*, GA 93a.

Choleric — one of the four *temperaments with a strong relation to the *'I' and to the *element of fire. People who have a choleric temperament have a strong awareness of their 'I', which expresses itself in blood circulation. They have a clear and quick overview of any situation in life, are born leaders and energetic organizers. Justice is extremely important for them and will be defended with fervour. An attack of blind anger is a possible danger, when the 'hot-headed' choleric does not know what he is doing and can inflict terrible damage without realizing it. Only after some hours, sometimes only the following day, will he realize

Choleric

what he has done; and then it will be possible to discuss it. When walking, the choleric tends to dig his heels firmly into the ground. His body is often strong and his neck short, almost hidden between shrugged shoulders. Cholerics are friendly as long as they are in command. Favourite colour is likely to be red.

Rudolf Steiner: *The Four Temperaments*, GA 57; *Discussions with Teachers*, GA 295.

Christ — highest divine being. When the 30-year-old *Jesus was baptized in the river Jordan by John the Baptist, Christ incarnated into the body of Jesus. In the Bible we read: '[...] and lo, the heavens were opened unto him and he saw the Spirit of God descending like a dove, and lighting upon him' (St Matthew 3: 16–17). For three years, Christ lived in this body until his death on the cross. In many ancient mythologies, Christ was seen as a divine being living in the *sun, who was to incarnate in a human body at some time in the future. By his incarnation Christ provided the *earth with new life. Since his 'descent into hell' and Resurrection, Christ has lived in the *ether body of the earth, and can be experienced by those who have developed the necessary supersensible perception. Christ is the origin, the purpose and the goal of our planet earth.

Rudolf Steiner: *The Gospel of St Matthew*, GA 123; *The Gospel of St Luke*, GA 114; *The Gospel of St Mark*, GA 139; *The Gospel of St John*, GA 103; Danielle van Dijk: *Christ Consciousness*.

Christian Community — the Christian Community was founded by the Lutheran theologian and minister Friedrich Rittlemeyer in Switzerland in 1922, with the support of Rudolf Steiner. The Christian Community is an independent Christian church centred on seven sacraments in a renewed form, with its own liturgy. There are some 350 Christian Community congregations worldwide. Although

22

not a field of work of anthroposophy as such, this church finds its inspiration in Rudolf Steiner's anthroposophy.

Evelyn Capel and Tom Ravetz: *Seven Sacraments in the Christian Community*.

Christmas — originally a pagan festival that has become a Christian celebration of the birth of *Jesus. According to Rudolf *Steiner there were two Jesus children. These two distinct children are described in the Bible in the Gospels of St Matthew and St Luke. The usual Christmas celebrations in the Christian world are a combination of the biographies of these two Jesus children, since one came from a poor family and was worshipped by the shepherds, while the other was of royal origins and was worshipped by the kings. As the western world came to celebrate the birth of Jesus, rather than the incarnation of Christ at the Jordan, the date on which we celebrate Christmas has shifted from its original date of 6 January (still celebrated by the Russian Orthodox Church) to 25 December, so that it is now linked instead to a physical birth, but also to the figures of Adam and Eve, who are celebrated on 24 December. Thus a subtle sense is preserved that Jesus redeems the Fall of Man.

Rudolf Steiner: *The Gospel of St Matthew*, GA 123; *The Gospel of St Luke*, GA 114.

Christmas Foundation Meeting — in German: 'Weihnachtstagung', when the General Anthroposophical Society was re-founded. This can be regarded as the rebirth of the Anthroposophical Society, first established in 1913. The Christmas Foundation Meeting took place in *Dornach, Switzerland, from 24 December 1923 to 1 January 1924. During this conference Rudolf Steiner laid the *Foundation Stone meditation into the hearts of the 700 or so people present, who had gathered in the joinery workshop next to the ruins of the *Goetheanum, which had burned

Christmas Foundation Meeting

down. Rudolf Steiner, who hitherto had not been a member of the Society, now aligned his personal karma with that of the renewed Society by becoming its chairman.

Rudolf Steiner: *The Christmas Conference*, GA 260; *World History in the Light of Anthroposophy*, GA 233; Rudolf Grosse: *The Christmas Foundation, Beginning of a New Cosmic Age*.

Christmas Play — the second in a sequence of three plays that are traditionally performed between *Advent and Epiphany by staff of many *Waldorf schools throughout the world. The complete sequence comprises the *Paradise Play, the Christmas Play, (subdivided into the Nativity Play and the Shepherds' Play), and the *Kings' Play. The plays were discovered in the nineteenth century by Rudolf *Steiner's teacher Karl Julius *Schröer in the village of Oberufer, in the border region between Hungary and Austria. The plays originate from an age-old tradition among local peasants who, with their folk humour and profound reverence, kept the plays alive. In the Christmas Play the story of the birth of *Jesus as described in the Gospel of St Luke is performed.

Rudolf Steiner: *The Festivals and Their Meaning*.

Christmas tree — in anthroposophical institutes, in *Waldorf schools and in family circles, the Christmas tree is decked out according to suggestions by Rudolf *Steiner. The tree is decorated with 30 red paper roses and three white roses round the top. The red roses represent the 30 years *Jesus lived on *earth before *Christ incarnated into him at the Jordan baptism. The three white roses represent the three years Christ lived in Jesus' body until his death on the cross.

The ancient signs of the *planets can be added as well, together with the alpha and the omega, representing Christ as the beginning and final goal of all Creation. Candles can be placed in the tree and a five-pointed star, a pentagram, may be put in the top of the tree as a symbol of Christ having become man. Many variations are possible, depending on local customs.

Rudolf Steiner: *The Festivals and their Meaning.*

Clairvoyance — the ability to perceive phenomena that are not noticeable to the usual *senses. Clairvoyance can be developed and occurs in various degrees, either less or more consciously controlled. Rudolf *Steiner was a very high *initiate with a high level of clairvoyance, which he was able to govern and consciously employ in inaugurating his spiritual science or *anthroposophy.

Rudolf Steiner: *Knowledge of the Higher Worlds*, GA 10.

Class readings — The School of Spiritual Science was established by Rudolf *Steiner in 1923 as the innermost core of the *Anthroposophical Society. Because of Rudolf Steiner's death soon afterwards in 1925, only the first class of this *Mystery school could be realized. Nineteen *esoteric lessons and a number of meditations were given. These lessons are read or rendered freely in regular meetings by specially trained class readers to members of the Society who are also members of the School of Spiritual Science.

Johannes Kiersch: *A History of the School of Spiritual Science, The First Class.*

Colour theory — Rudolf *Steiner's colour theory accords with that of Goethe (1749–1832). Goethe argued that colours originate from the interplay of light and darkness. Yellow originates from looking at light through darkness: the setting sun seen through the darkening atmosphere grows yellow and subsequently orange and red. Blue originates from looking at darkness through light: we look at the pitch-dark universe through the light of the sun and we see the blue sky.

Rudolf Steiner adds to Goethe's theory a colour division into *image colours* (green, white, black, peach blossom) and *radiant colours* (blue, red, yellow). The radiant colours are active, radiant like the light of the *sun. The image colours are passive like the sunlight reflected from the moon. This difference was elaborated in conversations Rudolf Steiner had with painters who were given directions for the specific use of these two types of colours. A wet-on-wet *painting technique is used in painting lessons in *Waldorf schools to give pure experiences of the colours' different qualities. The effect can be enhanced by painting the colours layer upon layer, in what is called *veil painting. Not only the painter but also those who look at the final picture can experience this process as healing. Attention is diverted to the creative forces behind the image itself, the intrinsic qualities of colour. In all fields of work inspired by *anthroposophy, this colour theory plays an important part in the use of colours in buildings, for instance in schools. Different coloured classrooms accord with the different types of consciousness of growing children.

Rudolf Steiner: *Colour*, GA 291.

Concept sense — see: Thinking.

Consciousness soul — that part of the *soul with which we can think about the act of *thinking. We observe the world with our twelve *senses and we first store all sensory impressions in our *soul. Next, we start thinking about these impressions. The third step is thinking about this thinking process.

In successive *cultural periods these stages are also clearly visible in the constantly developing human soul. Likewise, and in accordance with the *biogenetic law, every human being in his growth towards adulthood passes through the same stages. A baby is inundated with sense impressions. These are stored in the *sentient soul. While growing up, the impressions become increasingly differentiated through our thinking. The differentiated thoughts are stored in the intellectual soul. When adulthood is reached we acquire the self-reflective possibility of thinking about the thinking process: the *consciousness soul is born.

From a historical point of view it can be said that the consciousness soul was born at the start of the fifth post-Atlantean cultural period, around the year 1413. Renaissance and humanism may be regarded as expressions of this new configuration of the soul. This development continued through eighteenth-century rationalism and the Industrial Revolution to our modern age, in which information technology heralds a completely new stage of human consciousness.

Rudolf Steiner: *Theosophy*, GA 9.

Constitutional types — the classification of two constitutional types, the large-headed and the small-headed child, represents a principal division that is helpful when reflecting on individual children. In the large-headed child, the metabolic system strongly influences the nerve-sense organization. These children have a rich imagination and are not particularly open to sense impressions. They repose in themselves and are not easily disturbed. They have a tendency to daydream and usually have a stout physique. There is a link here to the *phlegmatic temperament.

In the small-headed child, the nerve-sense organization dominates the metabolic system. The head pole gives a solid and hard impression. Such children will be distracted by every sense impression, are likely to have a poor imagination and to be thin and pale. They are almost too adult-like. There is a link here to the *melancholic temperament.

Ideally, the two poles, the head with the nerve-sense system and the abdomen with the metabolic system and the limbs, are kept in balance. If this balance is lost all kinds of disorders may develop.

Rudolf Steiner: *Education for Special Needs*, GA 317; Husemann/Wolff: *The Anthroposophical Approach to Medicine*.

Cosmic intelligence

Cosmic intelligence — the intelligence originating from the
*hierarchies and guarded by the *archangel *Michael. This
all-embracing intelligence is the basis of all Creation. Due
to the necessary growth of individual powers of thought,
humanity was gradually cut off from awareness of this
cosmic intelligence. This development started in the ninth
century. Human beings acquired this intelligence but for-
got their cosmic origins. This new psychological stage can
be seen as a preparatory phase leading up to the birth of the
*consciousness soul in the fifteenth century. In other words,
after a long period of time during which human beings
received their thoughts as direct inspirations from the
*hierarchies, a new stage began when they could think by
and for themselves. *Anthroposophy tries to develop
awareness of cosmic intelligence as the hidden source of
our own consciousness.

Rudolf Steiner: *Anthroposophical Leading Thoughts*, GA 26.

Cultural periods — the term refers to the seven post-Atlantean
periods which are: *First,* Ancient India; zodiac sign Cancer
(7227–5067 BC). *Second,* Ancient Persia; sign: Gemini
(5067–2907 BC). *Third,* Egyptian/Babylonian Period; sign:
Taurus (2907–747 BC). *Fourth,* Greek/Roman Period; sign:
Aries (747 BC–1413 AD). In 1413 the present *fifth* post-
Atlantean period started, which has (at least as yet) no
specific name; this will last until 3573 AD; sign: Pisces.
These five periods will be followed by two more: the Russian Period; sign: Aquarius (3573–5733 AD); and the
American Period; sign: Capricorn (5733–7893 AD). These
cultural periods linked to the signs of the zodiac last about
2160 years each.

Rudolf Steiner: *World History in the Light of Anthroposophy*, GA 233.

Curative education — the anthroposophical approach to
caring for and educating children whose development has
been arrested or disrupted in some way. The curative

28

educator tries to enable the child's *'I' to manifest as much as possible. This 'I' itself is not damaged, but the child's body does not allow the 'I' to perform normal tasks. It is like a skilful musician trying to play a piece of music on a broken violin. It is a life-long task for such a human being to make the best of their limited capabilities. Curative education tries to unlock all dormant potential with the help of an artistic approach such as painting, curative *eurythmy or music. In curative education centres, rhythm is an important factor in guiding the 'I' of the child through time. Daily, weekly, monthly and yearly schedules and rhythms give a reassuring and stabilizing framework.

Rudolf *Steiner states that he has never come across a high *initiate who has *not* experienced a damaged *incarnation of this kind before reaching the initiation stage. This view sheds a truly valuable light on all the suffering that can be experienced in these cases. Rudolf Steiner also emphasizes the power of love that people with disabilities call forth from parents and educators.

Rudolf Steiner: *Education for Special Needs*, GA 317.

29

D

Desire — aspect of the *will originating in the *astral body.
Rudolf Steiner: *Theosophy*, GA 9.

Devachan — part of the spiritual world where the *'I' remains between two *incarnations. After death the 'I' initially remains in *kamaloka, after which its journey continues to 'lower devachan'. This lower devachan is the realm of the archetypes which, through the activity of creating spiritual beings, underpins the *minerals, *plants, *animals and *mankind. The extent to which the 'I' can observe these archetypal activities during its life between two incarnations depends on the affinity with these realms that was built up by the 'I' during the previous incarnation on *earth. The observations of the 'I' in the spiritual world help determine the character and quality of the subsequent life on earth.

After lower devachan, the 'I' arrives in higher devachan where it can meet these spiritual beings themselves and where the general plan for the following incarnation is designed. Then the 'I' returns to lower devachan where positive and negative relationships with fellow human beings are formed. This network of relationships will play an important role in the next life. Skills of observation and reflection developed on earth, as well as in the spiritual world between two lives, will help the 'I' in its overall development.
Rudolf Steiner: *Theosophy*, GA 9.

Devil — see: Lucifer.

Dichotomy — division in two, in this case referring to the belief that man consists of two parts: *physical body and *soul. Rudolf Steiner mentions the Council of Constantinople in 869 AD during which the Church Fathers decided that man consists of two and not of three parts — the *trichotomy of *physical body, *soul and *spirit. *Anthroposophy takes this threefold division for granted. The mind-body division was a philosophical tenet of Descartes, and has widely influenced subsequent views and outlooks.

Rudolf Steiner: *The Mission of the Archangel Michael*, GA 194; *Building Stones for an Understanding of the Mystery of Golgotha*, GA 175.

Dionysian — adjective of Dionysus, the ancient Greek god of wine. In *anthroposophy it refers to the disintegrating influence originating from the human metabolic system by means of which all food is broken down. Concepts such as 'movement', 'warmth' and 'chaos' define this field of energy. The limbs are considered to belong to the same field, which is also called the *will. This pole contrasts with the other pole linked to the ancient Greek god *Apollo, which is localized in the head.

Rudolf Steiner: *Study of Man*, GA 293.

Dornach — village near Basel, Switzerland. Centre of the *Anthroposophical Society and the School of *Spiritual Science at the *Goetheanum. Initial centres were Cologne and Munich in Germany. Due to the First World War, the Society moved to Dornach in 1913, where in the same year the construction of the first *Goetheanum started.

Rudolf Steiner: *Architecture, An Introductory Reader* (compiled by Andrew Beard, 2003, various GA numbers).

Dragon — collective name of all forces that try to distract human beings from their intended development. The dragon appears in many old stories and myths e.g. 'St George and the Dragon', the Song of the Nibelungs and *The Edda*. In the Bible we read about St *Michael slaying the Dragon. Rudolf Steiner relates how he was once told that, 'If you want to conquer the dragon you have to get into his skin'.

31

Dragon

In other words, we can only overcome adversary forces by getting to know them thoroughly. The feast of St Michael (29 September) is celebrated in *Waldorf schools and many other anthroposophical *fields of work. The story of St Michael slaying the dragon is often performed, and Michaelmas songs are sung.

Rudolf Steiner: *Knowledge of the Higher Worlds*, GA 10.

Dream — during sleep the *physical body and the *ether body lie in bed. The *astral body and the *'I' are temporarily in the spiritual world. Compared to the situation by day, the four *members interact in a completely different way. Dreams are one result of this, and arise at the threshold where astral body and 'I' leave or return to the ether and physical bodies. The degree of personal development of the astral body and the 'I' determines what kind of observations can be made while in this 'land of dreams', and Steiner describes how dream life changes as we engage in self-development. The dream can consist of images from the *etheric world, from the *astral world or from the world of *spirit. It can also be influenced by the physical body, if we eat certain foods before we go to sleep. Whether we wake up in the morning empty-handed or enriched by valuable impressions from our nightly sojourn in the spiritual world depends on our inner spiritual training, which can enable us to observe 'dreamland' surroundings of a higher kind.

Rudolf Steiner: *Anthroposophy and the Inner Life*, GA 234; *Sleep and Dreams*, GA 67.

Drugs — by using drugs we try to escape from our purely intellectual consciousness with its narrow boundaries. The *astral body and the *'I' are expelled from the *ether body and *physical body in an abnormal way. The 'I' is presented with deceptive illusions and has no control over these impressions. When the effects of the drug have worn off, the four *members reorganize in the usual way and a painful feeling of solitude can result. This unpleasant feeling invites the use of drugs again, eventually leading to addiction in which the 'I' has no control or governance.

When the various *cultural periods are closely studied, it appears that over time human consciousness has become increasingly cut off from the spiritual world, focusing instead on the *earth in its purely physical manifestation. In other words, the 'I' has become ever more embedded in the physical body. The 'I' can feel incarcerated in the physical body to such an extent that it starts looking for an escape route through drugs.

At the Council of Constantinople in 869 AD, the concept of *spirit was abolished. In the twenty-first century, the *soul is also now at risk from so-called 'western' ways of thought which do not acknowledge its reality. Only the physical body is left for the 'I' to identify with. However, we intuitively feel that we originate from a spiritual world, and some wish to force themselves into this world with the help of drugs, to seek reconnection with their spiritual homeland. Unfortunately, such a drug-aided and forced reconnection will not last long; and is soon replaced by a strong feeling of disappointment.

Rudolf Steiner: *True and False Paths in Spiritual Investigation*, GA 243; *From Elephants to Einstein*, GA 352; *Becoming the Archangel Michael's Companions*, GA 217.

Dynamic drawing — a subject taught in all years of the *Waldorf school curriculum, and also known as 'form drawing'. It develops from drawing simple shapes and forms, such as straight and curved lines in Class One, to complicated geometrical forms in the higher classes. In a non-intellectual way, involving and schooling all *senses, pupils engage creatively with geometrical laws and patterns. The eventual shapes on paper always represent the track of a certain movement. The spaces between lines are therefore, preferably, not coloured in. These movements, or gestures, can be recognized in the *formative forces of nature. Prior to the dynamic drawing lessons, the forms and shapes can be practised in a *eurythmy lesson during which pupils become acquainted with the form through their whole body. Dynamic drawing also supports the processes of learning how to write in the lower classes. Artistic forms from ancient cultures, such as Celtic or Greek, often serve as examples for dynamic drawing lessons in the higher classes.

Hermann Kirchner: *Dynamic Drawing;* Margrit Jüneman: *Painting and Drawing in the Waldorf School*; Gilbert Childs: *Steiner Education in Theory and Practice.*

Dynamis — spiritual beings belonging to the second *hierarchy, also called 'Spirits of Motion'. The continual movements in our *planet of water, air and of the planet itself, are expressions of this hierarchy. Continual metamorphosis in the *earth's vegetation is also caused by the Dynamis. In the term *'bio*dynamic*' the same concept, referring to the influence of the Dynamis, can be recognized.

Rudolf Steiner: *The Spiritual Hierarchies and the Physical World*, GA 110.

E

Earth — see: Planetary stages.

Easter — festival related to springtime in the northern hemisphere, when new life and growth occur in nature, and when Christ was resurrected from death. *Anthroposophy also draws attention to the *Resurrection of *Christ in the *ether body of the *earth. The resurrected etheric Christ nurtures this resurgence of life, and can be experienced by those who develop their perceptions in a special way. All ancient folk customs acquire a new perspective when this knowledge is taken into consideration. In the rhythm of the four seasons, spring is most suitable for celebrating this festival because it takes place when the planet is most receptive to Christ's life-giving force. See also: *Festivals.

Rudolf Steiner: *The Cycle of the Year*, GA 223; Danielle van Dijk: *Christ Consciousness*.

Electricity — similar to magnetism and nuclear power, electricity belongs to so-called sub-nature. Through the creative forces of the *harmony of the spheres, the spiritual world can condense into physical matter as we know it on *earth. Beyond a certain point, this densification process creates the realm of sub-nature, in which *Lucifer, *Ahriman and the *Asuras hold sway. Light *ether then becomes electricity. Sound ether becomes magnetism and life ether becomes nuclear power. The latter term is not used in *anthroposophy. However, in a lecture in Basel on 1 October 1911, Rudolf Steiner spoke of a force that is much stronger than any imaginable electrical discharge. He says that the human being's developing spiritual insight into the usual realms of nature should run parallel with his discoveries in this realm of sub-nature. Only when we are well-

35

Electricity

armed with spiritual knowledge of both can we meet
Lucifer, Ahriman and the Asuras without being over-
whelmed by these powerful forces.

Rudolf Steiner: 'The Etherisation of the Blood' in *Esoteric Christianity*,
GA 130.

Elemental beings — also called etheric elemental beings,
usually assigned to the four *elements of *earth, water, air,
fire. Among these beings are creatures such as dwarves
(earth), undines (water), sylphs (air) and salamanders (fire).
Our visible physical world is a modification of these invisible elemental beings. Just as invisible vapour can condense
to water, then, if the temperature drops further, solidify into
ice — or, in reverse, the ice can evaporate into thin air — so
all visible substances come into being by materialization of
these elemental entities. When these substances are
destroyed, the elemental beings are freed again. The
elemental beings are invisible to the untrained eye.

Rudolf Steiner: *Harmony of the Creative Word*, GA 230; Masaru Emoto:
The Hidden Messages in Water.

Elements — the classical four elements are: *earth (solid), water
(liquid), air (gaseous) and fire (warmth). In the first three
elements, the three states of aggregation can be recognized.
Warmth, or fire, is not seen as a separate state of aggregation
in modern physics. Each of the four elements is home to the
corresponding type of *elemental beings. *Christ, as the
sense and meaning of the world, is seen as the Lord of the
Elements. Considered in this way, planet *earth is a confluence of living beings that in themselves are supersensible
but whose existence gives rise to visible matter.

In *anthroposophy the four elements are, for instance,
mentioned in relation to the four *temperaments and the
four types of *ether.

Rudolf Steiner: *Harmony of the Creative Word*, GA 230; *Old and New
Methods of Initiation*, GA 210; J. L. Benson: *The Inner Nature of Colour*.

Entelechy — literally means 'containing its aim within itself'. The word 'intelligence' is derived from this term. A chestnut or a sunflower seed are each an entelechy because only a chestnut or sunflower can grow out of them. In the same way, the human being is an entelechy because the *'I', cloaked in its personal *karma, can only manifest in life on *earth what intrinsically corresponds to it. This definition sheds light on the fact that the human being is an intact and integral entity that passes through successive incarnations.

Rudolf Steiner: *The Threshold of the Spiritual World*, GA 17.

Esoteric — Greek, meaning: 'within', or 'hidden'. Rudolf Steiner has revealed a wide range of esoteric knowledge that hitherto had been preserved and passed on from *initiate to initiate through the ages in so-called *Mystery schools. This type of knowledge cannot be perceived or accessed with the physical senses. Rudolf Steiner has expressed this hidden knowledge in such a way that it became understandable to non-initiates as well. Those present at his lectures, and the readers of his books, could and can use their own power of thinking to absorb and assess the esoteric knowledge revealed.

Rudolf Steiner: *Foundations of Esotericism*, GA 93a.

Ether — in general, shapeless and invisible life force, also called the fifth essence or 'quintessence' in addition to the four *elements of earth, water, air and fire.

The following sequence shows how solid matter can melt, evaporate, change into warmth and, through the four kinds of ether, continue its way up into the spiritual world: *earth, water, air, warmth (or fire), warmth ether, light ether, sound ether, life ether*. The element of earth is considered to be the lowest, the most solid manifestation; and the life ether, at the other end of the scale, is considered to be the most highly evolved ether of a given entity.

The sequence applied to a tree, for instance, gives the

following picture. *Earth:* the physical tree. *Water:* the sap flowing through the bark, branches and the leaves. *Air:* the gaseous substances involved in the process. *Warmth:* the relative temperature of the tree. *Warmth ether:* keeps the tree alive for a certain period of time. *Light ether:* determines the size of the tree. *Sound ether:* causes the pattern of ramification. *Life ether:* encompasses and sustains the tree as a well-defined living entity. Through this modification process a spiritual concept can become manifest in the physical world.

Rudolf Steiner: *Anthroposophical Spiritual Science and Medical Therapy,* GA 313; Ernst Lehrs: *Man or Matter;* Ernst Marti: *The Four Ethers.*

Ether body — one of the four *members or bodies of the human being, also called 'life body' because it keeps *plant, *animal and *human being alive. At death, the ether body is separated from the *physical body. Due to this separation, the physical body falls into decay, since it cannot maintain its form by itself. Then the human ether body slowly dissolves into the general *ether of the *earth.

Ethereal forces can do their work best where fluids are available. This applies not only to the human body but to nature as a whole. Plants need water because only then can the ether forces keep the plant alive. A small wound in the mouth heals rapidly due to the abundance of saliva through which the ether forces can do their work. And on the beach, where we are surrounded by plenty of water, we can take in more life-giving ether forces than in the streets of a big town.

Ether forces also play a role in food. In the metabolic system, the ether forces present in vegetables, fruit, bread, etc., by means of which they have grown, pass on into the human ether body and eventually reach all four human *members, thus sustaining human life. Memory is another function of the ether body, since all habits and experiences are impressed into it. This function of the ether body therefore plays an important role in all learning processes. See: Change of teeth, Waldorf education.

Henk van Oort: *Anthroposophy, A Concise Introduction.*

Etheric aura — every living being, a plant, an *animal or *human being, has an *ether body which can be seen as a luminous configuration round the *physical body by people who have developed the necessary perception. The *earth as a living being also has an ether body of its own.

Rudolf Steiner: *Theosophy*, GA 9.

Etheric Christ — In the Bible, in Acts 9: 1–9, we read that Saul, Christ's persecutor, experienced an encounter with the etheric *Christ at Damascus. Saul sees a blinding 'light from heaven'. He hears a voice saying to him: 'Saul, why dost thou persecute me?' After this remarkable experience, Saul turned from being a persecutor to apostle of Christ. His name from then on was Paul, and he travelled to various countries to spread the Gospel. Rudolf Steiner tells us that the resurrected etheric Christ is present in the ether body of the *earth, and can be encountered by anyone who has developed the necessary perception.

Rudolf Steiner: *The Reappearance of Christ*, GA 118; Alfred Heidenreich: *The Risen Christ and the Etheric Christ*

Etherisation of the blood — clairvoyant perception shows a delicate ethereal flow from the human heart to the pineal gland in the head. This ethereal flow consists of etherised blood. This etherisation process takes place in and around the heart.

The phrase also refers to the event on Golgotha when the blood of *Christ flowed from his body on the cross into the *earth. The blood of Christ etherised and was united with the *etheric aura of the earth. In this process, the earth was rejuvenated with new life forces. The etherised blood of Christ, now present in the aura of the earth, can be united

Etherisation of the blood

with the human etherised blood that flows from the heart
to the epiphysis.

Rudolf Steiner: *The Reappearance of Christ*, GA 118; 'The Etherisation
of the Blood' in *Esoteric Christianity*, GA 130; *An Occult Physiology*,
GA 128.

Ether processes — in the *ether body, seven ether processes
can be observed. The terms mentioned below concern the
metabolic processes in the *physical body, the learning
processes of the *soul and the learning processes of the
*spirit. Teachers can shape their mode of teaching
according to these seven steps. The seven processes are:
Breathing: the food, the new impressions, etc. are taken in.
Warming: the *'I' starts to rework the new material in a
warming process. *Nourishing*: the new material has become
food for the 'I'. *Secreting* (or sorting): metabolism takes
place — the message and the carrier are separated. *Maintaining*: through practice, the newly acquired material is
individualized. *Growing*: the possibility of growth arises.
Reproduction: with the help of the newly acquired possibilities something entirely new can be produced.

Coenraad van Houten: *Awakening the Will*; Rudolf Steiner: *The Riddle
of Humanity*, GA 170.

Eurythmy — literally the word means: 'good rhythm'. Rudolf
Steiner inaugurated this new art of movement which can be
regarded as 'visible speech' or 'visible singing'. By means of
specific gestures the whole body is turned into a kind of
speech organ that manifests speech sounds. In the same
way, the body can represent sounds produced by musical
instruments, and thus musical compositions and human
speech can be brought to expression on the stage. At
*Waldorf schools, eurythmy lessons are given to all age
groups. These lessons connect poetry (through spoken
language), geometry (through gestures and the moving of
forms) and music (through rhythm, beat and melody).

A distinct and specialized form of eurythmy is used as therapy to address a wide range of health problems. There are post-graduate training courses in therapeutic eurythmy.

Rudolf Steiner: *Eurythmy as Visible Speech*, GA 279; *Eurythmy Therapy*, GA 315.

Evil — in general: a force that hampers the development of *mankind on *earth. From a wider perspective, evil turns out to be a force that stimulates any kind of development, both good and bad. We may wonder why the Tree of Knowledge, whose fruit Adam and Eve were not allowed to eat, grew in Paradise in the first place. Precisely because of this tree, man developed knowledge of his own situation and could evolve into a more or less self-aware creature (cf. The Book of Genesis). In *anthroposophy we come across two main adversary forces, *Ahriman and *Lucifer. Ahriman tries to persuade us that only the material world is true reality, while Lucifer tries to convince man that the spiritual world is the only true one. Between these two we must find our way towards true freedom. This process is given form in Rudolf Steiner's wooden sculpture 'The Representative of Humanity', in which Christ and the free human being are merged. See also: Asura.

Rudolf Steiner: *The World of the Senses and the World of the Spirit*, GA 134.

Evolution — the evolutionary theory of Charles Darwin (1809–1882) is considered by Rudolf Steiner to be intrinsically correct but to only partly describe the reality of evolution. In his anthroposophical cosmology, Steiner focuses on the initiating and organizing spiritual forces that were at work in evolution. One might say that Darwin closely studied the track a carriage left behind on a sandy path, but overlooked the driver and his motive for the journey. See also: Human being.

Rudolf Steiner: *Cosmic Memory*, GA 11.

Exoteric

Exoteric — public information or knowledge. Opposite of
*esoteric.

Exusiai — spiritual beings belonging to the second *hierarchy. Also called 'Spirits of Form'. In Hebrew the
equivalent of Exusiai is Elohim. They carried out the initial
plans of the first hierarchy that led to the creation of the
solar system and *mankind. The Elohim (a plural word) are
mentioned in the first lines of the Bible.

Rudolf Steiner: *The Spiritual Hierarchies and the Physical World,* GA
110.

Eyesight — one of the 12 *senses. Although the eye seems to
be a camera that only takes note of surrounding images in a
neutral fashion, the existence of optical illusions means that
the brain also interprets images. A trick of vision turns out
to be a trick of the brain. We are able to 'think' in our eyes,
so that in fact we only see the things we understand. We
send our inner spiritual light through the eyes into the
world where it is met by the light reflected from objects, in a
two-way system. In *Catching the Light,* Arthur Zajonc
writes: 'In 1910 an eight-year-old boy who had been blind
since birth was operated upon. After a successful operation
the boy could see but he was not able to interpret what he
actually saw. The two-way system had to be established
and practised in the years after the operation. In short: the
lights of nature and of mind entwine within the eye and call
forth vision.'

A. Soesman: *Our Twelve Senses*; Arthur Zajonc: *Catching the Light, the
Entwined History of Light and Mind.*

F

Fable — story in which *animals speak and act as human beings and in doing so display specific human characteristics. Fables and stories of saints form part of the storytelling curriculum of Class Two in *Waldorf schools. In fables, human beings are represented as personalities with a single overriding characteristic: as in every animal, only one determining quality has been developed. In stories of saints, on the other hand, human beings are represented as personalities who have overcome all forms of one-sidedness. Saints have learned to master all drives and impulses, as symbolized in pictures of saints surrounded by animals who seem to obey them. These saints are lord and master of their own *astral body. Both types of stories offer the child support as the astral body begins to emancipate itself. This process starts at about the age of seven and is concluded when the independent astral body is born with sexual maturity, at approximately age 14.

Rudolf Steiner: *The Education of the Child*, GA 34.

Fairy-tales — stories with ancient folk wisdom, passed on orally from generation to generation. Images from fairy-tales offer deep insight into a civilization's psychological and cultural development. In the nineteenth century many fairy-tales were collected to prevent them from being lost altogether as the oral tradition faded. Collectors included Alexander Afanasyev in Russia, Jean-François Bladé in France, Elias Lonnrot in Finland and Alexander Carmichael in Britain. The fairy-tales collected in Germany by the Grimm brothers are best known. Rudolf Steiner says of these fairy-tales that they were inspired by Christian *Rosencreutz and his school of

43

thought, and originate from the same spiritual background as *anthroposophy.

Rudolf Meyer: *The Wisdom of Fairy Tales*; Rudolf Steiner: *The Poetry and Meaning of Fairy Tales*, GA 62; Roy Wilkinson: *Interpretation of Fairy Tales*.

Fantasy — sometimes used in anthroposophic literature as synonymous with the concept of *imagination, although the word in general English usage has connotations of 'illusory'. In general, an intermediate state between daydreaming and the dream world of the night. The images of fantasy arise from the lower pole, the *will, connected with the metabolic system of the human body. This area is not directly accessible to our everyday consciousness.

However, when we are asleep, the *astral body and the *'I' are in the spiritual world. In this state, images inspired by the *hierarchies in the spiritual world can enter the lower pole, the will. On waking up, when the astral body and the 'I' re-enter the *ether body and the *physical body, these images can become manifest in our daily consciousness.

True imagination is the gateway from the spiritual world to the human physical world, and is evidence of the spiritual world becoming manifest in daily life. Use of the word 'fantasy' in this context is problematic, due to its connotations in English, and is not exactly synonymous with the German word *Phantasie* ('imagination').

Rudolf Steiner: *Autobiography*, chapter 15, GA 28.

Father — see: Trinity.

Feeling — from a physical point of view related to the chest, with the heart and the lungs, where *thinking and *will meet and rhythmically alternate. This alternation is represented by the beat of the heart and breathing in and out. Thinking occurs in a fully-awake state, whereas the will acts unconsciously. Feeling holds an intermediate position and thus unfolds in a dream-like state. This threefold division into: *thinking* (head) – *feeling* (chest with heart and lungs) — *will* (metabolic system and the limbs) — is an essential concept in the anthroposophic image of the human being.

In a child, feeling is strongly connected with the *will, with the digestive system. This becomes clear in drawings by very young children. In these drawings, a human being is initially represented like a *tadpole: a head with limbs. The middle section, the trunk, is missing. We can say that a child who draws these figures is still in a sleep-like state. As the child grows, the feeling realm develops between the realms of *thinking and *will, allowing thinking to develop independently into real awareness of the world.

Rudolf Steiner: *Study of Man*, GA 293.

Festivals — like towers in a landscape, the annual festivals mark important moments in the calendar as observed in *fields of work inspired by *anthroposophy. The main festivals are: *Easter, *Whitsun, *St John's, Michaelmas, *St Martin, *Advent, *Christmas, Epiphany. These festivals are not only reminders of events that took place in the past, but also reflect cyclical spiritual events that take place in the breathing process of the *earth every year. Due to their historical origins, these festivals relate to the northern hemisphere. The breathing process of the earth, however, is reversed in the southern hemisphere. For this reason, festivals celebrated there cannot necessarily follow the course determined by the northern hemisphere, but can instead be adapted to local circumstances.

Celebrating the festivals enables human beings to get in touch with both nature and *spirit. The annual cycle is not merely an endless repetition of the same festivals year after year. The festivals, if we engage with them fully and connect through them with our ongoing human evolution,

offer an opportunity for us to develop greater awareness of
the course and aim of human life on earth.

Rudolf Steiner: *The Festivals and Their Meaning; The Cycle of the Year*,
GA 223.

Fields of work — professional domains and areas of society in
which *anthroposophy plays an inspiring, innovative and
influential role. This is the case, for instance, in: *medicine,
*Waldorf education, *curative education, *biodynamic
agriculture and horticulture, *speech formation, *architecture, *eurythmy and *social science.

Henk van Oort: *Anthroposophy, A Concise Introduction.*

Fifth Gospel — in a series of 18 lectures, Rudolf Steiner
speaks of *The Fifth Gospel*, which is not, or is scarcely,
based on any related documents. Instead, the content was
drawn in a *clairvoyant way from the supersensible *Akasha chronicle which Rudolf Steiner was able to read. In *The
Fifth Gospel* we read about *Jesus' life between the ages of
12 and 30, a period hardly mentioned by the usual sources.
The innermost feelings of the apostles during Whitsuntide
(Pentecost), when the Holy Spirit was poured out upon
them, are also revealed (Acts 2: 1–17). The often incom-
prehensible facts mentioned in the four Gospels of the
Bible acquire a new, deeply spiritual background, so that
we can properly grasp them as modern human beings.
From the very beginning of Creation, *Christ is here shown
to have been inseparably linked to the development of the
*earth and mankind.

Rudolf Steiner: *The Fifth Gospel*, GA 148.

Folk spirit — see: Archangel.

Formative forces — in all earthly matter formative forces can
be detected, originating from spiritual sources which
themselves originate in the *harmony of the spheres. These
spiritual formative forces operate according to certain
laws. Rock crystal for instance always manifests a hex-

agonal shape. The same *six*fold tendency is seen in the flowers of all bulbous plants, whereas roses always have *five* sepals and cabbage has *four* petals in its cross-like (*Cruciferae*) flower. In a human being, the formative forces emanate from the head where *thinking is located. If the formative forces are too weak or cannot do their work for whatever reason, chaos will result. If the formative forces are too strong, life will fossilize and come to a standstill. This is the case in nature as well as in human thought processes.

Rudolf Steiner: *Harmony of the Creative Word*, GA 230; *Introducing Anthroposophical Medicine*, GA 312.

Form drawing — see: Dynamic drawing.

Foundation Stone meditation — given by Rudolf Steiner at the *Christmas Foundation Meeting in *Dornach, Switzerland, on Christmas Day 1923 to the 700 or so members of the *Anthroposophical Society present in the joinery workshop next to the remains of the first *Goetheanum, which had burnt down a year before. With the aid of the world of spirit, Rudolf Steiner laid this meditative foundation stone into the hearts of those present. Through this act, anthroposophy could from then on spread through the world as living spiritual light.

The Foundation Stone meditation encompasses the whole of anthroposophy, embodying spiritual reality linked to the *Trinity, the *hierarchies of *angels, and most clearly to *Christ. According to Rudolf Steiner, all who really live with the meditation will be able to receive this foundation stone of love into their heart.

The 'Foundation Stone meditation' concept also occurs in other settings. In many *fields of work inspired by anthroposophy, a foundation stone is laid when a new building is inaugurated. Usually a copper box containing a meditation written on parchment is laid in the foundations while building is in progress. This meditation will play a role in the spiritual life of the community that works in the finished building, such as a school or hospital.

Rudolf Steiner: *The Christmas Conference*, GA 260; Rudolf Grosse: *The Christmas Foundation, Beginning of a New Cosmic Age.*

Freedom — the concept is mentioned in the following quotation from chapter nine of Rudolf Steiner's book *The Philosophy of Freedom*: 'Nature makes of man merely a natural being; society makes of him a law-abiding being; only he himself can make of himself a free man.' The human being is not born as a '*tabula rasa*', a blank sheet. From previous lives he brings with him all sorts of tasks he has to fulfil in his present life. This inheritance is called *karma. Freedom arises when man can recognize his karma and consciously directs his *will to pursue this inevitable and necessary stream.

Rudolf Steiner: *The Philosophy of Freedom*, GA 4.

G

GA — *Gesamtausgabe* (German), referring to the Collected Works of Rudolf *Steiner, published for the first time in 1955 by the Rudolf Steiner Verlag, *Dornach, Switzerland. The GA includes approximately 350 numbered volumes consisting of:

1/ Written texts such as books, plays, essays, notes;

2/ lectures. Steiner gave approximately 6000 lectures, two-thirds of which were recorded in shorthand and subsequently published;

3/ works of art, such as poetry, meditations, paintings and drawings. There are various means available, including the internet, to explore this extensive legacy of spiritual knowledge.

Gilgamesh — see: Kali Yuga.

Gnome — see: Elemental beings.

God — referring to the Christian concept of the holy *Trinity, the three aspects of one godhead as *Father, Son and Holy *Spirit. The Trinity, as ultimate origin of the Creation of the world, inspires the *hierarchies of *angels.

The term 'god' is also used to define the inspiring spiritual powers of other cultures: Zeus (in ancient Greece), Ahura Mazda (ancient Persia), Brahma (India), Amun-Ra (ancient Egypt) and so on. Usually there is a connection with the *planets or the *zodiac. From a further and refined definition of these gods it becomes clear that the same gods appear under different names in various cultures. Gods also experience a certain development in themselves, due to which their outward appearance can alter. The concept of 'transparency' also plays a role: a god or an angelic being can temporarily act *through* another spiritual being.

God

*Anthroposophy sheds light on this complicated world of the gods and reveals the pattern of underlying connections.
Rudolf Steiner: *The Spiritual Hierarchies and the Physical World*, GA 110.

Goethe — 1749–1832, German lawyer, poet, scientist. Rudolf *Steiner was introduced to Goethe's works by K. J. Schröer who was Steiner's teacher at the Technical High School in Vienna. During private conversations about Goethe with Schröer, Steiner always felt the presence of a third person in the room, whom Steiner identified as Goethe himself. During his work at the Goethe and Schiller Archive in Weimar, Germany, from 1890 to 1897, Rudolf Steiner was greatly impressed by all that Goethe had achieved in his lifetime. Rudolf Steiner realized at a later stage in his own life that Goethe had helped him to focus on earthly matters. Without Goethe's inspiration Steiner, in his own words, would have been prematurely drawn to the spiritual world. Due to Goethe's 'admonishing finger', Steiner remained firmly grounded on *earth. Goethe said that the physical world and the spiritual world are to be seen as united and interwoven. In *anthroposophy the same unified concept is found.

Rudolf Steiner said of Goethe's fairy-tale, *The Green Snake and the Beautiful Lily,* that it describes the situation in the spiritual world at the period of the French Revolution. At that point the time had come for positive spiritual change to take place. The underground temple mentioned in Goethe's fairy-tale is raised up into the light of day for everybody to see — meaning that the spiritual world was open to all from that moment on. Unfortunately, things turned out very differently, and awareness of the spiritual world largely disappeared. However, Rudolf Steiner felt so closely connected to Goethe that he took up the threads of his work, incorporating Goethe's ideas into his own and

50

naming the Goetheanum after him, the *Anthroposophical Society's building in* Dornach, Switzerland.

Rudolf Steiner: *Autobiography*, GA 28; J.W. von Goethe: *The Fairy-Tale of the Green Snake and the Beautiful Lily*.

Goetheanum — building in *Dornach, near Basel, Switzerland. Centre of the *Anthroposophical Society and the School of *Spiritual Science. Building of the first, wooden Goetheanum, or 'House of the Word', was begun in 1913. It was destroyed by fire on New Year's Eve 1922/23. Rudolf *Steiner presented his model for the new, concrete Goetheanum in 1924. The Goetheanum hosts conferences, plays and concerts. The design of the building embodies *organic architectural principles.

Grail — an unequivocal definition cannot be given. Age-old stories tell of a stone that fell from *Lucifer's crown during a battle in heaven, as described in the Revelation of St John, the last book of the Bible (Revelation 12: 7–12). On *earth this stone, then serving as a chalice, is said to have been used to collect Christ's blood when he died on the cross. The chalice was then said to have been taken to England by Joseph of Arimathea when journeying to tin mines in Cornwall. This *exoteric story corresponds with a more *esoteric version in which the Grail may be regarded as the power of the etheric *Christ. After the Crucifixion at Golgotha, this power spread through the *ether bodies of all human beings, and has been called the *Grail stream. In stories of the Grail, physical and spiritual elements mingle and blend inextricably. The Grail stories were written down in the thirteenth century by Chrétien de Troyes, Robert de Boron and Wolfram von Eschenbach.

Rudolf Steiner: *Christ and the Spiritual World: The Search for the Holy Grail*, GA 149; *The Mysteries of the Holy Grail* (various GAs); Danielle van Dijk: *Christ Consciousness*

Grail stream — one of the four *mystery streams on which

Grail stream

*anthroposophy is based. From a European perspective the Grail stream originated in the East and moved to Europe during the various successive *cultural periods. Religious and *esoteric content from ancient India, ancient Persia and the ancient Graeco-Roman period gave shape to this mystery stream. Following unification of the four mystery streams at the *Christmas Foundation Meeting in Dornach in 1923/24, *anthroposophy can be called the science of the *Grail.

Walter Johannes Stein: *The Ninth Century and the Holy Grail*; Sergei O. Prokofieff: *Relating to Rudolf Steiner*; B.C. Lievegoed: *Mystery Streams in Europe and the New Mysteries*.

Group soul — *plants and *animals have a group soul that does not manifest in the physical world. The *initiate with specially trained perception can observe these group souls. Only parts of the group soul — the plants and animals themselves — incarnate on *earth. In earthly circumstances these parts are subject to an ageing process, eventually die and are replaced, while the group soul remains constant in the spiritual world of archetypes. Steiner described this as fingers poking through a wall, seemingly separate but in fact united in one, unseen hand. In a distant past, human beings had a group soul as well. For this reason people in the past tended to look much more alike than nowadays. After the development of their independent *'I', human beings incarnate more completely on earth, adapting their physical bodies and facial expressions to their distinct inner field of influence.

Rudolf Steiner: *The Christian Mystery*, GA 97; *True and False Paths in Spiritual Investigation*, GA 243; *Harmony of the Creative Word*, GA 230.

Guardian of the threshold — there are two guardians of the threshold: the lesser guardian and the greater guardian. The lesser guardian reveals itself as a being created by man himself during previous *incarnations and the present one.

Through this being man can meet, recognize and understand his own *karma. The *threshold exists because, if arriving in the spiritual world unprepared, man would be unable to bear all the responsibility for his own deeds. Only when man can do so, will he be able to engage consciously with his own destiny. The lesser guardian guides man through this process. On the journey in the spiritual world between two incarnations, he sees to it that man has enough understanding to proceed on his way. The concept of the 'doppelgänger' (double) approximately coincides with the lesser guardian. The difference is that the 'doppelgänger' can appear in a more or less spontaneous way, for instance after a serious accident, and that the lesser guardian appears after spiritual training. The Swiss psychiatrist C.G. Jung uses the term 'shadow' to indicate the phenomenon of the lesser guardian.

The next step on this spiritual road is the encounter with the greater guardian who urges man to deploy on earth all his acquired knowledge and capacities to benefit his fellow creatures. Only when he does so can he enter the spiritual environment in which the greater guardian lives. Every night when going to sleep, man has a chance to meet the greater guardian if he offers up spiritual content for him to carry into supersensible realms. If man only takes impressions from the physical world into his sleep, the greater guardian must bar his way into the spiritual realms. The greater guardian is identified as *Christ

Rudolf Steiner: *The Threshold of the Spiritual World*, GA 17.

H

Harmony of the spheres — the ancient concept that the physical world originated from the formative music of the spiritual world is described in the works of Pythagoras (582–507 BC) and is taken up by many philosophers after him. The harmony of the spheres is also mentioned by John Dryden (1631–1700): 'From harmony to harmony this universal frame began'; and by William Shakespeare (1564-1616) in his play *The Merchant of Venice*: '... such harmony is in immortal souls, but whilst this muddy vesture of decay does grossly close us in, we cannot hear it.'

This music of the spheres in not audible in the usual way but can be understood conceptually in terms of mathematics. Ernst Chladni (1756–1827) has shown, with his so-called *Chladni figures, that sound can produce all kinds of patterns in loose sand on a flat plate, when this plate is made to vibrate with a bow. The pitch of the sound causes a related figure. Chladni's pioneering work is taken further by Alexander Lauterwasser, who shows the same formative power of sound with the help of modern technology. Masaru Emoto is working along the same lines: his photos of freezing water show a multitude of ice crystals, the shape of which depend on the quality of the water sample, any surrounding music, and even on human thoughts. In *anthroposophy the term *'sound ether' is used to denote the same process. Spiritual formative forces shape solidifying physical matter through sound. See also: Logos.

Rudolf Steiner: *Harmony of the Creative Word*, GA 230; Masaru Emoto: *The Hidden Messages in Water*; Alexander Lauterwasser: *Water Sound Images, The Creative Music of the Universe*.

Hearing — one of the 12 *senses. Hearing enables us to find inner balance between all everyday auditory impressions. The connection between the ear and the sense of balance is not only obvious in the physical organ but is expressed in language as well. We must be able to stand, physically and mentally, to really *under*stand. Hearing is the first level at which spoken language penetrates our consciousness. It also plays a role in our spatial awareness. By hearing all sorts of sounds around us we can assess our own location and position. The sense of hearing can also reveal the true character of an object. For instance, a blind man in a shower of rain can tell what materials the rain is striking.

Rudolf Steiner: *Study of Man*, GA 293; Albert Soesman: *Our Twelve Senses*.

Heart — in the triad *thinking, *feeling and *will, the heart is linked to feeling. The heart and the lungs fulfil an inter-mediate function between the head (thinking) and the digestive organs and the limbs (will). In the heart, the two capacities of *thinking and *will meet during breathing in and breathing out; mediating between them, the heart and lungs keep a healthy balance between these faculties. In contrast to the usual concept of the heart, *anthroposophy tells us that it beats *because* blood flows through the body. The heart is thus not an organ that pumps the blood around us, but instead responds to the living circulation of the blood. The blood circulates in blood vessels through the action of the *ether body, the *astral body and ultimately the *'I'. In this sense, the heart may be regarded as an extremely sophisticated sense organ, mediating between contrary forces and responding dynamically to all levels of the organism including supersensible ones.

Rudolf Steiner: *Therapeutic Insights*, GA 205.

Hierarchies — there are nine groups of spiritual beings at a higher level than *humankind. They are subdivided into three groups of three. The division is as follows: third

Hierarchies

hierarchy (closest to the human being): *Angels, *Archangels, *Archai. Second hierarchy: *Exusiai, *Dynamis, *Kyriotetes. First hierarchy (closest to the Holy *Trinity): *Thrones, *Cherubim, *Seraphim. From all accounts by Rudolf Steiner it appears that these hierarchies were closely involved in Creation in the distant past. They still guide the *metamorphic process that *humankind and the cosmos undergo on their linked evolution to the next *planetary stage of our solar system, the 'New Jupiter'. By undergoing this metamorphic process, mankind will eventually become the tenth hierarchy. This process may be seen as the aim of life on *earth.

Rudolf Steiner: *The Spiritual Hierarchies and the Physical World*, GA 110.

Higher 'I' — see: 'I'.

History — in general: the development of human consciousness through the ages. *Anthroposophy sheds light on the coherence of consecutive stages of human consciousness. This ever-changing consciousness is expressed in the sequence of different civilizations from the distant past through to the present day. Historical facts and dates can be seen in an entirely new perspective when *karma and *reincarnation are taken into consideration. Historical events become more comprehensible and acquire real depth when the corresponding spiritual background is revealed. History then appears not as a merely random sequence of events but as the expression of an underlying, purposeful plan. Humankind turns out to be the central axis of the overall *evolution of planet *earth.

Rudolf Steiner: *World History in the Light of Anthroposophy*, GA 233.

Holy Nights — the 13 nights between *Christmas and Epiphany, on 6 January. During winter the dark side of the *planet holds its breath, so to speak. Life forces have been breathed in and are active within the earth. The *elemental beings in the earth are busy preparing the coming spring with its new resurgence of life. People on this wintry side of the earth can experience a deepening of dream life. From a spiritual point of view, experience can intensify during these 13 nights and we can awaken more profoundly to the world of *spirit. Such an experience is described in *The Dream Song of Olaf Åsteson*, an ancient folk tale from Norway.

Rudolf Steiner: *The Cycle of the Year*, GA 223.

Holy Spirit — see: Trinity; Whitsun.
Human being — see: Mankind.
Humankind — see: Mankind.
Hyperborea — see: Planetary stages.

I

I — the immortal and inalienable core of a human being. Through *reincarnation, the 'I' travels from one life on *earth to another and can also be identified as an *'entelechy', a word from which 'intelligence' is derived. (Entelechy comes from the Greek and means: 'containing its aim within itself'. For instance, an acorn is also an entelechy because only an oak will grow out of it.) The word 'individual', meaning 'indivisible', is another definition of the 'I'.

*Anthroposophy makes an important and clear distinction between the higher 'I' and the lower 'I'. The higher 'I' remains in the spiritual world during an incarnation on earth. It is the author and coordinator of our biography and can be compared with the conductor of an immense orchestra. What we feel as our 'I' during our life on earth is the mirror image, or 'ego', of this higher 'I'. The ego is an accumulation of past experiences in life on earth. This link with planet earth also appears from the word 'ego'. It is a combination of two Greek roots: 'e' (out of) and 'go'(earth). The more someone identifies with his ego or lower 'I', the more difficult it becomes to gain awareness of the purely spiritual entity of this higher 'I'. As soon as this dual nature of the 'I' is discovered, inspiration can be drawn from the higher 'I', realizing that *humankind is of spiritual origin and that life on earth is one part of our existence in recurring incarnations, along with intervening sojourns in the world of spirit. In anthroposophy, the higher 'I' is seen to be related to *Christ.

Rudolf Steiner: *A Psychology of Body, Soul and Spirit*, GA 115.

Imagination — referring to the first stage of *initiation and related to the faculty of *thinking. As distinct from the ordinarily understood meaning of this word — the capacity to see pictures in our mind that are not necessarily 'real' — in anthroposophy imagination is a capacity for true perception. *Clairvoyant imaginative perception may occur without direct understanding. After undergoing spiritual training, imaginations can reveal their significance. Imaginations form the basis of the whole physical world and can be seen as the spiritual 'plan' behind the physical world. They may be compared to the initial plan of an architect who starts designing a house. Everything physical in this world is a solidified modification of spiritual imaginations. The observer of an imagination is in touch with the sphere of action of the third *hierarchy. If someone perceives an imagination, he can be simultaneously aware of a physical object and the spiritual 'plan' behind this object. See also: *inspiration and *intuition.

Rudolf Steiner: *Anthroposophical Leading Thoughts* nos. 29, 30, 31, GA 26.

Imitation — essential activity during the first seven-year period of human life: a developmental stage in which the child fully imitates his surrounding world. This process puts great responsibility on the shoulders of parents and teachers. Educators are real examples in every way. The child imitates not only outward actions and words of those around him but also their moral stance. In *Waldorf schools, teachers use this innate capacity throughout the first school years in finger games and all kinds of movement activities that come into play as a preparation for writing, reading and arithmetic. The child enhances his bodily and spatial awareness through these activities. The brain 'listens' to what the limbs carry out and is thus further structured. This neuroplasticity has recently been confirmed in brain research. The discovery of *mirror neurons as the physical basis of this imitation process confirms what Rudolf *Steiner stated about imitation and its effect on the nervous system and the brain. These contemporary discoveries also highlight the interrelation of the lower and the upper *senses. See also: Will.

Rudolf Steiner: *Study of Man*, GA 293; *Practical Advice to Teachers*, GA 294; Daniel Siegel: *Mindsight*.

Incarnation — human embodiment of an *'I' that originates from the spiritual world (incarnate = coming into the flesh). Rudolf *Steiner gave many examples in his lectures on *karma and *reincarnation of successive incarnations of well-known people. When a series of incarnations of the same 'I' is revealed, a whole new concept of the human being can arise. Hidden connections suddenly become comprehensible and aspects of history acquire a new dimension.

Rudolf Steiner: *Manifestations of Karma*, GA 120; *Reincarnation and Karma*, GA 135.

Incorporation — a spiritual being can invade a human being to such an extent that the *'I' of that human being is pushed aside. This spiritual being uses the human body for its own ends. The aim of such an incorporated spiritual being can vary widely from evil to good. It must be said that the term 'incorporation' is sometimes used to denote *'incarnation', and it is important to distinguish between these two concepts.

Initiate — one who has been initiated. See: Initiation.

Initiation — the revelation of hidden spiritual concepts to human beings who can understand and pass on this *esoteric knowledge. Through all ages, hidden spiritual truths have been guarded and passed on to the following generation by *initiates such as priests, pharaohs, shamans, monks and so on. Such esoteric knowledge had always been safeguarded carefully, to prevent it being tainted by ignorance or misused by adversary spiritual forces. However, Rudolf *Steiner, himself a high initiate, revealed much of this esoteric knowledge in all his lectures and writings as times had changed, and it was now right for ordinary people to gain access to such knowledge. In former times, initiation involved the entwining of personal elements with perception of the spiritual world. *Anthroposophy as a new form of initiation aims at a completely objective perception by the independent *'I' of the world of *spirit.

Rudolf Steiner: *Mystery Centres*, GA 232; *True and False Paths in Spiritual Investigation*, GA 243; Danielle van Dijk: *Christ Consciousness*.

Inspiration — second stage of *initiation relating to the faculty of *feeling and to the *heart and lungs with their rhythmic processes. The *initiate at this stage can perceive the living flux from which *imaginations come into being. As well as imaginations themselves, the hidden source of these imaginations will also become apparent as the activity of spiritual beings. At this level, the initiate is in touch with the sphere of the second *hierarchy. See also: Imagination; Intuition.

Rudolf Steiner: *Leading Thoughts* nos. 29, 30, 31, GA 26.

Instinct — aspect of the *will originating in the *physical body.

Rudolf Steiner: *Study of Man*, GA 293.

Intuition — third stage of *initiation linked to the *will and the *metabolic system. At this stage the initiate is able to perceive not only the activity of spiritual beings but those beings themselves who initiate all creative processes. At this level the initiate also experiences his own previous *incarnations. He is in touch with the sphere of the first *hierarchy. See also: *imagination and *inspiration.

Rudolf Steiner: *Leading Thoughts* nos. 29, 30, 31, GA 26.

I-sense — with this *sense the *'I' of someone else can be perceived. If we really look someone in the eyes we are searching for their 'I'. The very short movements of the eyes from left to right and back again while looking at someone is related to this intensive search. During such a close observation we try to 'look through' the physical body as if it were transparent, in search for the real individuality of the other.

Albert Soesman: *Our Twelve Senses*; Rudolf Steiner: *The Study of Man*, GA 293.

Isis — deity from Ancient Egypt who states: 'I am the All. Nobody has ever lifted my veil.' Rudolf *Steiner suggests this message could be revised and renewed as: 'I am the All. I am the past. I am the present. I am the future. Every mortal must lift my veil.' This means that with *anthroposophy the time has come when the veil of the physical world should be lifted so that we once again perceive the spiritual origin of the physical world. Rudolf Steiner has opened up ancient, hidden mysteries because the dark era — *Kali Yuga — came to an end at the end of the nineteenth century, and henceforth humanity's return to the spirit can begin.

Rudolf Steiner: *Ancient Myths*, GA 180.

J

Jesus — Rudolf *Steiner casts a clarifying light on the diverse and irreconcilable contradictions between accounts given in the four Gospels of the life and teachings of Jesus. If the information in the Gospels is related not to one child but to two different children, many contradictions in the story disappear. To really understand Rudolf Steiner's view of the two Jesus children some knowledge of the fourfold view of the human being is necessary (physical body, ether body, astral body and 'I'). The Jesus child mentioned in the Gospel of St Matthew descends from the royal line of King Solomon, whereas the Jesus child in the Gospel of St Luke descends from Nathan the priest. From Rudolf Steiner's information about the four *members of the two Jesus children, it appears that the spiritual world had been working for long ages to create a very special human body — one that would eventually enable *Christ to incarnate on *earth. Siddhartha Gautama as *Buddha, and *Zarathustra as *Ahura Mazda's priest, also played a part in this remarkable process. The four bodily sheaths of the two Jesus children merged at a certain stage, to create the body in which Christ could incarnate and live for three years until his crucifixion. Rudolf Steiner's Christology offers immense insight into these events, which our present *consciousness soul now longs to understand.

Rudolf Steiner: *The Gospel of St Luke*, GA 114; *The Reappearance of Christ*, GA 118.

Jupiter — the name of the present planet in our solar system but also the name of the next planetary stage of the *earth. Rudolf *Steiner calls the earth the 'planet of wisdom' which is to be transformed into the 'planet of love' or the 'new

Jupiter

Jupiter'. The 'substance' of this new Jupiter will be love. This transformational *esoteric process is going on in the four human bodily sheaths or *members. The three lower members, *physical body, *ether body and *astral body are being transformed by the *'I' into three higher members: *spirit man, *spirit self and *life spirit. Within these higher members, the 'I' will be able to continue its evolution through this new earth embodiment. See also: Planetary stages.

Rudolf Steiner: *Occult Science, An Outline*, GA 13; *Theosophy*, GA 9.

K

Kali Yuga — the dark era which, according to Rudolf
*Steiner, lasted from about 3000 BC until 1899 AD. The term
derives from Hinduism. During this era humankind
gradually lost contact with the spiritual world. This was
necessary to allow a sense of separate individuality and self-
reliance to evolve. In humanity's history, examples can be
found of this fundamental change of consciousness. At the
beginning of this dark era we find the Gilgamesh epic from
the Egyptian-Babylonian *cultural period. Gilgamesh
cannot understand the death of his friend Enkidu (or
Eabani in recent versions). In other words, Gilgamesh is
now unable to perceive the *soul of his friend in the spiritual world after he has died. Before the start of Kali Yuga,
human beings could penetrate the spiritual world relatively
easily, and report their experiences after returning to the
*physical body. Another example of being cut off from the
spiritual world is the difficulty people in Egypt increasingly
experienced in understanding their own dreams. This is
shown in the biblical story of Joseph, who is summoned to
explain the pharaoh's dreams.

At the end of Kali Yuga in 1899, it started to become
easier for human beings to perceive the spiritual world
again, though now with their newly acquired, conscious
*'I'. *Anthroposophy arrived at the end of this dark era,
and draws on new possibilities and capacities for recon-
necting our spiritual aspect with the spirit in the cosmos.

Rudolf Steiner: *The Reappearance of Christ*, GA 118.

Kamaloka — Sanskrit: 'place of desire'. After death, the *'I' is
presented with a panoramic view of the life that has just
ended. Then follows the kamaloka stage in which the *soul

Kamaloka

has to experience the torment of the desires it still has but cannot satisfy, because it no longer has the physical organs to do so. This period lasts about one third of the life that has just come to an end. It is the time one has spent in sleep during life on *earth. Dante, in his *Divine Comedy*, calls this period 'Purgatory'. Not only does man relive his own desires, but also the positive and negative emotions which he caused his fellow human beings. In this purification process the *'I' comes to understand how its own development was hampered. The results of this purification process flow into the next life. When the soul has cleansed itself, the kamaloka period comes to an end and the soul ascends to the following stage, called *'devachan'.

Rudolf Steiner: *Founding a Science of the Spirit*, GA 95; *Theosophy*, GA 9.

Karma — sanskrit: 'deed', especially related to the concept of cause and effect. Karma and *reincarnation are often mentioned simultaneously as deeds in a certain life have an effect on the following life. We are not born on *earth as a '*tabula rasa*', a blank sheet. On the contrary, from previous lives we take with us the results and conditions that play a formative role in a new life. Karma has various levels. First there is biological karma related to the inherited *physical body and the *ether body that sustains it. The inherited physical body facilitates all our actions yet also limits them at the same time. Secondly, there is psycho-social karma related to an extensive range of motives and qualities in the *astral body. Thirdly, there is biographical karma related to the *'I'. In his lectures Rudolf *Steiner gave many examples of various incarnations of well-known people to illustrate how karma works. From these sequences, underlying karmic interconnections become clear, with all their causes and effects.

Knowing oneself is greatly aided by getting to know

66

one's own karma. As soon as the various karmic levels at work are recognized, man can form a clearer picture of the aim of his life.

Rudolf Steiner: *Manifestations of Karma*, GA 120; *Reincarnation and Karma*, GA 135.

King's Play, The — the third in a sequence of three plays performed at *Waldorf schools between *Advent and Epiphany (on 6 January). The Kings' Play represents the events that took place after the birth of *Jesus, as described in the Gospel of St Matthew.

Rudolf Steiner: *The Festivals and Their Meaning.*

King Winter — personified seasonal image drawn from the *elemental world, like Jack Frost though clearly of more regal origins! In the kindergarten and lower classes of the *Waldorf school, the seasonal table is decked out with a winter landscape in the midst of which King Winter and his castle of ice are enthroned. The king is clad in white and may be served by snow elves who bring him snow crystals. Somewhere in a dark corner of the classroom, Lady Thaw and Lady Rain are hiding and awaiting their chance to come and wash away the ice and the snow. By such means, young children are helped to connect more deeply with the forces active in nature. For some weeks this tableau can play an important role in the stories told to a class, with many subjects such as writing and reading being linked to these seasonal stories.

Rudolf Steiner: *Harmony of the Creative Word*, GA 230.

Kyriotetes — spiritual beings belonging to the second *hierarchy. Also called 'Spirits of Wisdom'. They carry out what the first hierarchy has initiated through the creation of our solar system and *humankind.

Rudolf Steiner: *The Spiritual Hierarchies and the Physical World*, GA 110.

L

Language sense — one of the 12 *senses, also called the sense of speech. With this sense we can identify a sequence of sounds as meaningful language, combining the musical spectrum of the sounds of separate letters, in order to grasp the word spoken. The same takes place in a child who has just started reading. He can pronounce the separate letters 'c', 'a', 't', as soon as the sound-sign link has been established. But another step is required to inwardly 'hear' the word 'cat' as a whole. The sense of language also supports our grasp of grammatical structures.

Rudolf Steiner: *Study of Man*, GA 293; Albert Soesman: *Our Twelve Senses*.

Leading Thoughts — see: Anthroposophical Leading Thoughts.

Lemuria — period in the solidifying development of the *earth in which the present moon separated from the earth. The Pacific, with its ring of islands and volcanoes, is probably the area from which the moon mass left the earth. After this event, the earth's crust hardened gradually. The human being, whose *physical body was then still malleable, was open to cosmic influences, and more or less hovered in the very young, liquid and gaseous atmosphere of the earth. At a certain stage, man was able to inhale divine substances to create separate interiority, thus becoming distinct from the substances in which he had been living until that moment. At this period, differentiation of the sexes into male and female also occurred. The story of Paradise in the Bible gives an account of this development, as well as of the human being coming to know the difference between good and evil and thus becoming a real inhabitant of the earth. Unfortunately, evil forces at work in human beings gained the upper hand and, as a result of this, the continent of Lemuria disappeared in turbulent volcanic activity into the earth's crust See also: Planetary stages.

Rudolf Steiner: *Occult Science, An Outline*, GA 13.

Life sense — one of the 12 *senses. This sense informs us of our physical condition and of feelings such as hunger, thirst, pain, tiredness, etc. Feelings of boredom, impatience or irritation also have a physical effect and are perceived by this sense. The life sense ensures a correct balance between *physical body, *soul and *spirit. Sensing the life processes in our body enables the *'I' to engage in performing its healing and harmonizing work.

Rudolf Steiner: *Study of Man*, GA 293; Albert Soesman: *Our Twelve Senses*.

Life spirit — during life on *earth, the four bodily sheaths or *members of the human being, the *'I', *astral body, *ether body and *physical body, act continuously on one another. During this process, the 'I' very gradually transforms portions of the three other principles. The part of the ether body transformed by the 'I' is called life spirit. This humanized part of the ether body does not dissolve after death, but accompanies the 'I' into the spiritual world during its journey between two incarnations. When the 'I' is born again, the life spirit continues to grow until, after further lives, the whole of the ether body has been transformed entirely into life spirit. The astral body and the physical body undergo a similar process. In the end, man will transform entirely into a spiritual being, continuing to evolve at the following *planetary stage of the present *earth, called the new *Jupiter. See also: Spirit man; Spirit self.

Rudolf Steiner: *Theosophy*, GA 9.

Light — condensed modification of spiritual principles. In reality, it is neither a collection of particles nor an energy of a certain wavelength. On its way from the spiritual world to earthly matter, light modifies through various stages in which the level of condensation increases. Light is the first form of corporeality. Light in itself is invisible. From studies on the relationship between the human eye and light it appears that the act of seeing is a two-way dynamic in which human beings merge inner light from the eyes with outer light that the eyes receive. From the ensouled science of *Goethe and Rudolf *Steiner, it can be concluded that light is the garment of the *Logos, or the divine Word.

Arthur Zajonc: *Catching the Light, The Entwined History of Light and Mind.*

Logos — see: World-word

Lord of Karma — term coined by Rudolf *Steiner, defining one of the aspects of *Christ. It will rest with Christ to decide how our karmic account, with its credit and debit sides, will shape our lives in future incarnations. Christ taught people to forgive. If people forgive their fellow human beings, the need for karmic redress disappears, and cosmic energy is freed. Each deed of forgiveness creates a free space in the karmic web. This liberated energy is used to give shape to the next developmental stage in which our planet *earth will evolve — the new *Jupiter.

Rudolf Steiner: *From Jesus to Christ*, GA 131; Sergei O. Prokofieff: *The Occult Significance of Forgiveness.*

Lotus flower — see: Chakra.

Love — 'Love is to the world as the sun is to life on earth.' 'Love is the moral sun of the world.' These two definitions by Rudolf *Steiner refer to the comprehensive, cosmic-divine power of love. It was with this source of love that *God created the world. If we open up to this power of love we can be creative in every sense of the word. Every deed performed out of selfless love creates a free karmic space in the following *incarnation, which undoes the need for recompense or redress. This faculty of love eventually comes into its own if humankind unites unselfish love with the wisdom already present on earth. *Christ, who descended from the spiritual world, realized this unity of love and wisdom on earth. From this newly created substance of love will arise the next planetary stage of the earth, the new *Jupiter. By performing deeds of unselfish love, we contribute to this far-reaching process.

Rudolf Steiner: *Love and its Meaning in the World*, GA 143.

Lucifer — from Latin, 'light bearer'. An angelic being involved in Creation from the very beginning. Lucifer still exerts a strong influence on *humankind. Because man was intended to be a being with an independent *'I', the holy *Trinity allowed this counter-force in Creation. If this adversary power had not existed, mankind would never have been able to distinguish between good and *evil. At the present stage of the earth's evolution, Lucifer tries to dissolve all physical things. He tries to prematurely establish a spiritual realm of his own elsewhere. We can experience the influence of Lucifer whenever we find our attention is drawn away too much from earthly matters: if we are too absorbed in the arts or too involved in religion, or end up daydreaming. However, luciferic forces should not be regarded as solely negative. These forces provide great gifts and are necessary in human development but they must be kept in balance. The opposite force to Lucifer is *Ahriman, who wishes to shackle us to all things physical as the sole reality. *Christ holds a balancing position between Lucifer and Ahriman, as depicted in Rudolf *Steiner's large sculpture of 'The Representative of Humanity'.

Rudolf Steiner: *The Influences of Lucifer and Ahriman*, GA 191.

71

M

Macrocosm — the presently known universe originating in the Holy *Trinity and created by the *hierarchies. All physical *matter throughout the universe is the result of condensing spiritual concepts emanating from spiritual beings. Stars are colonies of spiritual beings as are the planets of our solar system. Physical matter does not come into existence by itself but is the result of creative spiritual forces that have a clear aim. These macrocosmic spiritual forces find their reflection in the microcosm of the *earth, in the four realms of nature: *minerals, *plants, *animals and *mankind, the latter embodying a culmination in which these two principles interpenetrate, as Steiner describes extensively in his *Occult Science*. From the ancient idea of 'as above, so below', Steiner elaborates highly complex and detailed insight into the manifold interconnections and reflections between the macrocosm and the microcosm.

Rudolf Steiner: *Occult Science*, GA 13.

Magnetism — see: Electricity.

Manas — the part of the *astral body that has been transformed by the *'I' during life on *earth is called manas or *spirit self.

Mankind — after the minerals, *plants, and *animals, *mankind is the fourth kingdom in nature. Humankind was present from the beginning of Creation, when the *hierarchies, in realizing the impetus of the *Trinity, created Ancient *Saturn. Mankind can be recognized as the central intent in this complex creative process. Minerals, plants and animals can be identified as early separations from the evolving human *entelechy, which gradually descended from the spiritual world into earthly conditions. This human entelechy materialized only after the minerals, plants and animals had appeared on *earth. This ancient course of development is mirrored in that of every child who is conceived, grows in the womb and is born. Studying embryonic development and birth can help understand the birth of mankind as a whole, which is not only the result of evolutionary development on earth but of a creative process that occurred supersensibly, in the spiritual world. A very broad perspective shows that, from the beginnings on Old Saturn, mankind is evolving through seven planetary stages to become the tenth *hierarchy. See also: Evolution.

Rudolf Steiner: *Occult Science*, GA 13; Hermann Poppelbaum: *Man and Animal, Their Essential Difference.*

Manu — the ancient initiated leader of humanity who led people from *Atlantis, before it sank into the present Atlantic Ocean, through Europe and Asia to safer territory in today's India, where ancient Indian culture (7227–5067 BC) was established. Noah in the Bible and Utnapishtim in the *Gilgamesh Epic probably refer to the same leading *initiate. See also: Cultural periods.

Rudolf Steiner: *Spiritual Hierarchies and the Physical World*, GA 110.

Matter — modification of spiritual concepts. All that arises in material and temporal conditions originates in the eternal. In the same way that invisible vapour condenses into water and eventually can coagulate into solid ice, spiritual concepts are transformed into visible matter. This process is also described in texts on the four kinds of *ether. See also: Maya.

Ernst Lehrs: *Man or Matter*; Ernst Marti: *The Four Ethers.*

Maya — Sanskrit: 'illusion'. The Oriental is inclined to say that the physical world is maya, unreal, a veil of illusions, whereas the Westerner, in general, holds that the spiritual world is unreal illusion. *Anthroposophy tries to make clear that the physical world is a modification of the spiritual world. Rather than a Platonic separation of physical and spiritual worlds, the concept of nature propounded in anthroposophy is based on *Goethe (1749–1832) who taught that nature is an 'open secret' in which the two worlds meet and interact. Both worlds exist, each in their own right. The extent to which this confluence can be perceived depends on our own developing capacities of perception.

Rudolf Steiner: *The Spiritual Hierarchies and the Physical World*, GA 110.

Medicine — the suggestions Rudolf *Steiner gave for further developing medical science were put into practice by the Dutch doctor Ita *Wegman. Anthroposophic medicine is practised worldwide by university-trained, fully-qualified doctors who, besides using orthodox medicines and methods of treatment, also prescribe anthroposophic medicines prepared according to Rudolf Steiner's indications. Knowledge of the four human *members or bodily sheaths is essential for understanding anthroposophic medicine. If these four members are not in harmony with each other and with the environment, illness is likely to occur. Anthroposophic medicine tries to support and stimulate the self-healing powers present in all of us. Anthroposophic doctors often collaborate with therapists working with the same approach. In some countries, anthroposophic health care has developed to the extent of providing anthroposophic treatment in specialized clinics. One example of such a clinic is the Lukas Klinik for cancer care and treatment in Switzerland.

Rudolf Steiner/Ita Wegman: *Extending Practical Medicine*, GA 27; *The Healing Process*, GA 319.

Meditation — seen as a personal matter and not usually practised in groups. In some countries, people who meditate on a regular basis engage together in meditation workshops in which they discuss and support each other's meditative practice. Besides meditation on feeling-imbued and often Christian-related images or texts, there are many meditative verses and exercises recommended by Steiner for developing, for example, tranquillity, courage, an inner connection with the seasons (see *Calendar of the Soul) or a connection with those who have died. In addition, Steiner provided a series of so-called *'supplementary exercises' for mastery of thought, feeling and will, which ensure that meditative practice does not become one-sided or dangerously remote from real life. Meditation can be seen as a way to connect the spiritual nature of the human being with the spirit in the cosmos.

Rudolf Steiner: *Verses and Meditations*; *The Stages of Higher Knowledge*, GA 12; *A Way of Self-Knowledge*, GA 16; *The Calendar of the Soul*, GA 40; Rudolf Steiner: *Meditations* series (various GAs).

Melancholic — one of the four *temperaments. Although there are many aspects, the following can be said about this temperament in a general sense. Of the four human *members or bodily sheaths — the *physical body, the *ether body, *the astral body and the *'I' — the physical body dominates the other three in those of a melancholic temperament. The *element of *earth, with all its characteristics, has the upper hand. Someone with a melancholic temperament is strongly aware of the weight of the physical body and all its gravity-related limitations. The physical body with the skeleton is felt as a heavy burden, giving a tendency to focus on life's problems and difficulties. Sorrow is intensely felt and joy much more rarely. Favourite colours may be brown and black. While this temperament can lead to isolation and loneliness, every temperament has its positive aspects, and melancholics have the potential to develop great compassion for the sufferings of others and maintain lifelong friendships. Teachers and parents of melancholic children are advised to provide much warmth and understanding. See also: Choleric; Phlegmatic; Sanguine; Temperament.

Rudolf Steiner: *Discussions with Teachers*, GA 295.

Members of the human being — also called bodily sheaths. Minerals have one member: a *physical body. *Plants have this plus an *ether body. *Animals have three members: physical body, ether body and *astral body; while human beings have all these plus a fourth, the *'I'.

Rudolf Steiner: *Theosophy*, GA 9; *The Education of the Child*, GA 34.

Memory — in ancient times, when human beings were clair-voyant and the four *members were not yet as closely interconnected as nowadays, memory as such was not needed. There was no need to store sense impressions because they were always at hand through *clairvoyant perception. Not only the present but also the past was available by reading in the so-called *Akasha Chronicle. In due course, as the four members became more closely intertwined, clairvoyance increasingly faded and eventually disappeared altogether. Personal memory therefore became necessary. The first stage was a localized memory system, related to place and occurrence. People created statues, rock paintings or inscriptions to record and remind themselves of a certain event. At a second stage, they employed rhythm in spoken texts to support their memory functions. At a third stage memory became fully inter-nalized. In silence, without any memory aids, people gradually acquired the capacity to memorize all kinds of sense impressions. This is the present situation. The ether body is nowadays largely integrated into the physical body, more or less coinciding with it rather than extending beyond it as in older times. The *ether body in the child is closely involved in growth of the physical body in the first seven years, then emancipates itself somewhat from these processes with the *change of teeth, and becomes more available to support memory. In child development, historical evolution of memory systems is repeated. In the early years, for instance, nursery rhymes based on rhythmic and regularly repeating words engage with a child's rhythmic memory, and objects or pictures from a *fairy tale can be displayed in the classroom to remind children of a particular story, as 'localized memory'. Rhythm has also traditionally been used for memorizing multiplication tables.

Rudolf Steiner: *Study of Man*, GA 293; *Practical Advice to Teachers*, GA 294.

Metabolism — see: Will.

Metamorphosis — change of form. This notion plays an important role in the anthroposophic concept of *evolution. To acquire real understanding of Creation, it is important to become aware of the continually changing forms in nature. Ever new impulses from the spiritual world change the visible world in every way. Metamorphic sequences can be discovered, for example in the vortices and flow of water, or in the forms of human or animal vertebrae. These have been used as the basis for sculptural 'flow forms' which re-energize water, with all sorts of practical uses such as sewage purification. In another scientific domain, Lawrence Edwards closely studied and recorded planetary influences on changing leaf bud forms. It is relatively easy to observe the changing forms of growing plants, animals and human beings, but more difficult to observe the gradual transformation of the whole earth and the cosmos. Even more complex is the metamorphosis that *humankind undergoes from the early beginnings on Old *Saturn through to the *Vulcan stage. *Reincarnation can also be regarded as a metamorphic process in our *biography, by means of which we slowly transform into a more spiritual existence.

Rudolf Steiner: *Cosmic and Human Metamorphoses*, GA 175. Lawrence Edwards: *The Vortex of Life.*

Michael — the *archangel who from 1879 acts as the *spirit of the age, until the year 2300. According to old legends, Michael, with his shining sword, cast out Satan from heaven, after which the latter continued life amidst *mankind on *earth as the 'dragon'. The dragon does not just confront us from without, but lives within us also, for instance as a starkly materialistic outlook. St Michael and *anthroposophy are connected in a special way. As the custodian of cosmic intelligence, and as spirit of the age, Michael inspires all human beings who wish to connect the human spirit with the spirit in the cosmos. *Anthroposophy is also called the School of Michael. Rudolf Steiner sought to establish a new festival of Michaelmas, at the end of September, to celebrate human qualities of courage and fortitude. Michael, with his 'sword of iron', has a special relationship with cosmic iron, with the iron in human blood, and the meteor showers that fall in greater number at that time of year. He stands sentinel over the human potential for freedom, waiting for free human deeds but not dictating how this should be achieved. See also: Kali Yuga.

Rudolf Steiner: *Anthroposophical Leading Thoughts*, GA 26; *The Apocalypse of St John*, GA 104; The Bible: Revelation 12: 7–12.

Microcosm — see: Macrocosm.

Midnight hour — the phrase is used to refer to the moment in higher *devachan, in the spiritual world between two earthly lives, when the *'I' finally takes leave of its previous life and starts preparing the next life on *earth.

However, the phrase is also used to refer to an event that many *initiates of the ancient *Mysteries experienced, whether in India, Persia, Egypt or Greece, during which they were introduced to the invisible spiritual forces of the sun. These forces can be identified with *Christ. On the shortest day of the cold season in the northern hemisphere, initiates were led into a completely dark chamber in which they could experience 'the *sun at midnight'. At the moment of vision, all matter was obliterated and the sun of the spirit, or Christ, radiated through the darkness of matter. In their inmost being, initiates gave birth to Christ in their higher self at that moment. This event developed into the Christmas festival as we still know it today.

Rudolf Steiner: 'Winter Solstice' in *Verses and Meditations*; *Festivals and their Meaning*; Sergei O. Prokofieff: *Rudolf Steiner and the Founding of the New Mysteries.*

Minerals — formed in ancient times, reminders of cosmic forces originating from the 12 signs of the *zodiac. These forces participated in the creation of the *earth and are still manifest in nature. The forces present in minerals are used in producing anthroposophic medicines, and in making *preparations for *biodynamic agriculture.

Knowledge of these cosmic forces has been present in all ages, and for this reason we find minerals in such things as crowns, sceptres and rings. Such gems are said to serve as mediators between cosmic forces and the human bearer of a precious stone. There are supersensible associations between minerals, the zodiac and *planets, and our physical organs, *senses and faculties.

Mirror neurons — when someone sees somebody else carrying out a movement or a gesture, the same neural circuits in the brain of both people will fire. These neural circuits are called mirror neurons. For instance, if we see somebody fall or otherwise hurt himself, our mirror neurons react immediately and enable us to feel a sense of the pain in a reflective fashion. In less conspicuous movements, the mirror neurons also react but we are unaware of the effect.

Mirror neurons

The activities of the mirror neurons vary between people. In some they act and react strongly while others find it difficult to 'read' or reflect someone else's body language or psychological experience.

Mirror neurons were discovered in 1996 during an experiment with monkeys at the University of Parma, Italy. Rudolf *Steiner describes the same effect, though in other words, in his tenth lecture of *Study of Man* (1 September 1919), given to the teachers of the first *Waldorf school in Stuttgart, Germany. In teaching, use can be made of the function of the mirror neurons, especially where young children are concerned. Children are great imitators. Not only do they immediately imitate the gestures of finger games, for instance, but also subconsciously reflect a teacher's language, opinions and body language. Rudolf Steiner emphasized how children imitate every aspect of the adult world and how educators can use this fact when teaching. See also: Imitation.

Rudolf Steiner: *Study of Man*, GA 293; Daniel Siegel: *Mindsight*.

Moon — see: Planetary stages.

Moon node — the moon node is an astrological term referring to the intersection of the moon's orbit with the ecliptic (= the sun's apparent orbit). The concept of the moon node is connected with the moment of birth, and the cosmic impulse relating to the positions of the *sun, moon and *earth. This same position is repeated every 18 years, 7 months and 9 days. A moon node can make itself felt in life as a major and suddenly occurring shift. On such an occasion we can reconnect with our prenatal decision to incarnate and our deeper purposes in doing so. We gain another opportunity to consider why we came to earth, and to configure our life in accordance with this prenatal resolution.

Rudolf Steiner: *Mystery of the Universe*, GA 201.

Mother Earth — also called Gaia, and closely related to Demeter, the Greek goddess of agriculture. The *earth is seen as the feminine aspect of Creation, and the surrounding cosmos as the masculine aspect. Mother Earth appears in many guises in ancient myths and *fairy-tales throughout the world. In children's stories she represents the life-giving forces in nature, and is often assisted by 'root children', representing the *elemental world. On the seasonal nature table in many *Waldorf schools, Mother Earth, with her root children, is seen to adorn nature with fresh leaves and colourful flowers. Rather than merely fanciful or sentimental, this aims to convey to children a deeper sense of the earth as a nurturing sentient being or organism who in turn needs nurturing. This accords with the ideas of some modern scientists such as James Lovelock (the 'Gaia theory').

Sibylle von Olfers: *The Story of the Root Children*; Heather Jarman: *Mother Earth's Children.* James Lovelock: *Gaia: A New Look at Life on Earth.*

Movement, sense of — with this *sense we become aware of the movements of our own body. The movement of a hand for example only happens as it should when we can perceive the movement precisely. For example, the idea and intention of moving one of our hands springs from the *'I' and is passed on to the *astral body, then on to the *ether body and eventually to the *physical body. If the movement cannot be fully realized via our *nerves, for whatever reason, an incomplete movement will result. If we hold one of our hands out of sight, behind our back for example, the sense of movement also tells us if the hand is flat or clenched.

This sense also plays a role when we observe the shapes and movements we see in everyday life around us. Inwardly we imitate every shape and every movement we observe.

Movement, sense of

The recently discovered *mirror neurons form the physical basis of this remarkable process.

Rudolf Steiner: *Study of Man*, GA 293; Albert Soesman: *Our Twelve Senses*.

Mysteries, the — ritual actions usually performed by priests during which access is gained to the hidden world of spirit. In all cultures, such Mysteries played an important role in giving impetus to evolving cultural development. The rituals in the Mysteries were secret affairs. If these secrets were betrayed, the betrayer might be killed to prevent carefully guarded wisdom falling into the wrong hands. Rudolf *Steiner has revealed much of this hidden wisdom because it was his conviction that the time had come to bring these teachings into the open. In *anthroposophy, the ancient Mysteries before *Christ's birth are considered to prefigure the Christian Mystery of Christ's resurrection.

Rudolf Steiner: *Mystery Centres*, GA 232.

Mystery plays — between 1910 and 1913 Rudolf *Steiner wrote a sequence of four mystery plays: *The Portal of Initiation, The Soul's Probation, The Guardian of the Threshold* and *The Soul's Awakening*. The plays represent the experiences of the *soul during Christian *initiation. Through this process the *soul is able to discover its higher *'I' and its connection with *Christ, learning the true significance of Christ's resurrection in the *earth's etheric sphere. The plays show how the characters are connected on the physical as well as the spiritual plane. Virtually all aspects of *anthroposophy are introduced in these plays. If nothing but these plays were to survive, stated Steiner, the essential teachings of anthroposophy would be preserved. They were first performed in Munich in 1910.

Rudolf Steiner: *Four Mystery Dramas*, GA 14; *The Presence of the Dead on the Spiritual Path*, GA 154.

Mystery streams — the four Mystery streams are cultural

currents from four different spheres of the compass and flow together in *anthroposophy. They are:

1/ The northern stream, also called *Vidar stream*. This stream inspired pre-Christian, Germanic culture, reflected in *The Edda*, an epic which extensively describes the Germanic pantheon of gods and heroes;

2/ the eastern stream, also called the *Grail stream*. This stream inspired Ancient India, Ancient Persia and Ancient Greece. The Mystery of Golgotha and the *Grail are part of this stream;

3/ the southern stream, also called the *Rosicrucian stream*. Ancient Egypt, the Templars, Ancient Rome and its continuation in the Roman Catholic Church are part of this stream;

4/ the western stream, also called the *Arthurian stream*. The Celts, Ireland, and the legendary King Arthur are part of this stream.

   Rudolf *Steiner sought to unite these four Mystery streams through the *Christmas Foundation Meeting in *Dornach in 1923. This unification inaugurated the new Mysteries as embodied in anthroposophy.

Rudolf Steiner: *World History in the Light of Anthroposophy*, GA 233;
B.C.J. Lievegoed: *Mystery Streams in Europe and the New Mysteries.*

Mysticism — a path that leads to the supersensible world through contemplation and self-surrender. In general it can be said that a mystic tries to acquire *initiation by finding the ultimate reality either within himself or in nature. The anthroposophic path of initiation tries to unite both these, as expressed in the anthroposophic endeavour to unite art, religion and science, raising subjective experience by disciplined means into an objective tool of cognition in which feeling is not dismissed as unscientific, but included as an objective mode of enquiry. We cannot understand the world either by simply 'looking within' nor through supposed 'objective' analysis of phenomena. Reality can only be grasped fully by invoking all complementary human capacities of *thinking, *feeling and *will. In the past, Creation was unconsciously seen as a whole. After a long period and necessary processes of evolution, during which scientific consciousness developed and focused entirely on the material world, this unifying outlook is again possible to heal the rift between ourselves and nature, although now in a conscious way through the autonomous and self-reliant *'I'.

Rudolf Steiner: *Mystics After Modernism*, GA 7.

Myth — a story passed down through the ages which embodies a certain stage or cycle in the development of human consciousness. From explanations that *anthroposophy can give about many myths, it appears that human consciousness is not a fixed attribute but a purposeful sequence of evolving states of consciousness, from the beginning of Creation on Old *Saturn through to *Vulcan.

Rudolf Steiner: *The Influence of Spiritual Beings on Man*, GA 102.

N

Nation spirit — *archangel from the third *hierarchy that leads a population and endows its language. In the *Edda* we read how Odin gives the Northern European population their language. The linguistic formative force of a nation spirit appears in the sound qualities and etymology of a language. In the English word 'tree' the vertical force from root to crown is emphasized, whereas in the Dutch 'boom' and the German 'Baum' we gain an impression, rather, of the solid girth of a trunk and branches, with the enveloping canopy of the leaves. The same idea is present in the English 'beam' which has the same etymological root. The activities of an archangel as nation spirit are also expressed in the general character and disposition of a people, and their historical destiny.

Rudolf Steiner: *The Influence of Spiritual Beings on Man*, GA 102; *Universe, Earth and Man*, GA 105.

Nerve — The nerves sense all activities of the *astral body, such as emotions, hunger, thirst, intent — for instance, the intention to take a book from a table. These activities in the astral body are transferred to the *ether body and the *physical body, a process that eventually results in movements which actually take the book from the table. The intent comes first, the movement follows. When an arm or leg cannot be moved due to paralysis, the person involved is not able to sense that part of the body. The astral body is then unable to connect with the ether body and the physical body corresponding to the paralysed part. If we compare the astral body with the strings of a puppet, it can be said that in such a case these imaginary strings do not function properly. This situation sometimes inadvertently happens when the circulation of the blood is hampered somewhere: we say that our leg has 'gone to sleep'. The leg is not felt and cannot be moved until the blood circulates freely again and the astral body can connect once more with the ether body and the physical body.

In the polarity of *blood and nerve, the nerve represents a dying process. The nerve has a tendency to become part of the *skeleton whereas blood represents life and has a tendency to evaporate into spirit. When the nerves are exposed to too many sense impressions, tiredness is felt due to this dying process.

The *sense and the nerve centres are primarily located in the head in contrast to the metabolic system in the abdomen, with its greater flow of blood. In Genesis, the first book of the Bible, these two poles are mentioned as the *Tree of Knowledge* (the head) and the *Tree of Life* (the abdomen). Only when the two poles are well balanced can a state of health be maintained. Too much use of the *Tree of Knowledge* will wither the *Tree of Life*; and vice versa, excessive life forces make it hard to keep a 'cool head' that can easily reflect and think. See also: Thinking.

Rudolf Steiner: *Study of Man*, GA 293.

Nuclear energy — see: Electricity.

O

Occult — hidden, *esoteric, known only to the *initiated. In spite of the fact that *Goethe called nature an 'open secret', much knowledge about the spiritual world is not readily or easily accessible. Only those who have developed the necessary spiritual perception have access to the world that is the source and origin of the visible world. Rudolf *Steiner has revealed much occult knowledge because he was convinced that mankind was ready to receive it. The relatively new *consciousness soul, combined with the end of *Kali Yuga, enabled his audience to absorb much spiritual insight. His listeners sometimes had the feeling, during his lectures, that the spiritual world rushed in on them, almost stupefying them. Others objected to the revelation of spiritual truths that had been hidden so long, and accused Rudolf Steiner of divulging age-old wisdom from the *Mysteries. His early audiences were not used to hearing such esoteric subject matter. One of Steiner's early works was entitled *Occult Science,* and gives a huge panorama of spiritual knowledge including a comprehensive account of *planetary stages and *human evolution.

Rudolf Steiner: *Man in the Light of Occultism, Theosophy and Philosophy*, GA 137; *Guidance in Esoteric Training*, GA 245.

Organic architecture — although the term does not specifically indicate anthroposophic architecture, Rudolf *Steiner's guidelines for architecture were profoundly organic. Organic architecture, though made manifest in rigid building materials, creates awareness of the dynamic spiritual formative forces in nature. Because the design is intended to be alive and natural, the 90° angle is avoided wherever possible. An organic building follows the laws of

Organic architecture

a living organism rather than of fixed building materials. In moving through such a building, we experience a rhythmic and often *metamorphic sequence of doors, windows, corridors, halls, stairwells, etc. *Anthroposophy takes for granted that all forms we see leave an imprint on the four human *members or bodily sheaths, as proven also by the recently discovered *mirror neurons. In this way, organic architecture enlivens us in body, soul and spirit considerably more than straight lines ever can. Many buildings related to anthroposophy's *fields of work have been designed in this way. One of the first buildings created in this style is the *Goetheanum in *Dornach, Switzerland.

Rudolf Steiner: *Architecture as a Synthesis of the Arts*, GA 286.

P

Painting — in *Waldorf schools, the 'wet-on-wet' painting technique is used with younger children. The paper is first moistened and placed on a board. Then the painting is done with watery paint and a broad brush, after which the paint slowly dries into shapes and forms. The method is used to give children a direct experience of colours and their different qualities and characteristics — as opposed to drawing with wax crayons or coloured pencils, where images are more easily defined and delineated. The effects of the colours are strongest when the paint is still wet, and the process and experience of painting is more important than the finished result.

Later on, children are introduced to the technique of *veil painting, in which many layers of thin, watery paint are applied successively. Patience is required between each layer since the colour must dry before the next 'veil' is painted. This technique creates a surprising effect in which the layers of colour become translucent and luminous, as if released from the paint itself. Both techniques reflect the way in which earthly matter can resolve into *ether quality and, vice versa, how ether can solidify into earthly substance. This effect raises awareness in both painter and observer of ethereal life processes, and the dynamic reality of a non-physical colour world.

Rudolf Steiner: *Colour*, GA 291; *Practical Advice to Teachers*, GA 294.

Palm Sunday — the Sunday preceding *Easter, which commemorates *Jesus' entry into Jerusalem riding on a donkey, on a road adorned with palm branches. (Mark 11: 1–11 and John 12: 12–16). This event is often celebrated in the lower classes of *Waldorf schools in a festival that interweaves pagan and Christian elements. The children make a cross of two sticks and decorate it with garlands of boxwood, nuts and sweets. In the middle of the cross a circular twig is attached as a symbol of the *sun. A hen, made of bread, is placed atop this as a symbol of vigilance. The children then walk through the school with their palm sticks, singing songs about springtime and *Easter. The procession can be extended by visiting an old people's home in the neighbourhood.

Rudolf Steiner: *The Festivals and Their Meaning.*

Panorama — the first experience after death is a detailed and vivid panorama of one's past life. People who have had a near-death experience often mention such a film-like panorama. The phenomenon is caused by the fact that the *ether body loosens itself from the *physical body. Gradually it dissolves into the general ether body of the *earth, and all past experiences that have been stored in the personal ether body are revealed to the *'I' as a sequence of images appearing in reverse order from the moment of death back to the moment of birth.

Rudolf Steiner: *Between Death and Rebirth*, GA 140.

Paradise Play — the first of three plays from Oberufer, Austria, that are traditionally performed at *Waldorf Schools and in other anthroposophical *fields of work between *Advent and Twelfth Night on 6 January. The play shows how Adam and Eve are expelled from the Garden of Eden, as described in Genesis.

Rudolf Steiner: *The Festivals and Their Meaning.*

Parzival — a central figure in medieval epics, and a great initiate. Various names (Percival, Parcival) exist, as do versions of his story composed by authors such as Wolfram von Eschenbach (1170–1220) and Chrétien de Troyes (1135–1190). Belonging to the *Mystery stream coming from the East, Parzival unites this stream with the Western

90

stream when he becomes king of the *Grail after many trials and tribulations. The central question he learns to ask eventually, having initially failed to do so, is 'What ails thee?' In other words, his mission is at least partly to develop interest and compassion in others. Parzival can be regarded as a human representative of *Michael, who seeks to realize Christ's impulse on earth.

Rudolf Steiner: *Christ and the Spiritual World: The Search for the Holy Grail*, GA 149; *The Mysteries of the Holy Grail* (various GAs).

Pedagogical law, the — a law formulated by Rudolf Steiner, according to which one member or bodily sheath of a teacher or parent affects the next lower member of the child. For example, if the educator wishes to work on the child's *physical body, he should do so through his own *ether or life body. If he wishes to focus on the child's ether body, then the educative impulse must flow from or through his own *astral body. Likewise, to influence the child's astral body, he should work out of his *'I'. To work on the 'I' of an adolescent one needs to work out of one's own higher 'I'. This process may also occur among adults, for instance between social worker and client.

Rudolf Steiner: *Education for Special Needs*, GA 317.

Person — or personality. Derived from Latin 'personare', meaning 'sound through'. In ancient times, actors used to wear masks, the *persona*, through which they spoke the lines of a particular character. In the modern anthroposophic sense of the word, a 'person' is a *human being through whom the *'I' sounds. Or more precisely: the lower 'I' is identical with the person, or persona, through which the higher 'I' can manifest

Rudolf Steiner: *Theosophy*, GA 9.

Perspective — perspective in the pictorial arts developed in the fourteenth and fifteenth centuries. Previously, artists seemed unaware of the laws of perspective — development

Perspective

of human consciousness mirrored in the growing child approximately at age 10. In both cases this step can be seen as a step forward towards greater awareness of the physical world, as detached from the observer. The discovery of perspective by the child serves as a signpost to teachers and parents of a new stage in the child's development towards adulthood.

Rudolf Steiner: *The Renewal of Education*, GA 301; *Discussions with Teachers*, GA 295.

Philosophy of Freedom, The — see Freedom.

Phlegmatic — one of the four *temperaments. The phlegmatic temperament is connected with the functioning of the *ether body and the *element of water. Someone with a phlegmatic temperament is liable to be comfortably self-contained, yet spread mentally into his surroundings like a lake. Self-awareness and a sense of time are less well developed. The metabolic system exerts great influence on thinking faculties, and so consciousness is partly drawn to the lower pole, the *will. Phlegmatics enjoy food, especially soft and sweet foods. In class a phlegmatic child can be a wonderful centre of calm and quiet. Their favourite colour is often blue. Too much of the phlegmatic temperament can lead to indolence. Phlegmatics are very hard to rouse to anger, but when they do become angry it can be profound and volcanic.

Rudolf Steiner: *The Four Temperaments*, GA 57.

Physical body — in a general sense referring to the earthly modification of spiritual concepts. These spiritual concepts become manifest in a condensed shape and form according to prevailing earthly circumstances and, in the case of humans, according to *karma as well. All four realms of nature — *minerals, *plants, *animals and *human beings — become visible to the physical senses in a physical body. Minerals consist of a physical body only. Plants have a physical body and an *ether body. Animals have a physical body, an ether body and an *astral body. Human beings have a physical body, an ether body, an astral body and a spiritual entity, usually called the *'I'.

Rudolf Steiner: *Study of Man*, GA 293; *Harmony of the Creative Word*, GA 230; Henk van Oort: *Anthroposophy, a Concise Introduction*.

Planet — The planets of our solar system, the *sun included, were once united in one celestial body. Through a complicated development, initiated and guided by spiritual forces, the present solar system acquired its form (see Planetary stages). The orbits of the present planets can be regarded as the sphere of influence of ancient planetary conditions in which spiritual beings are still present, from there contributing to the *evolution of the *earth and its creatures.

Rudolf Steiner: *Occult Science*, GA 13.

Planetary seals — to decorate the hall in which the Theosophical Congress in Munich was held in 1907, Rudolf *Steiner designed seven columns. Each column was related to one of the traditional seven planets (*Sun, *Moon, Mars, Mercury, *Jupiter, *Venus, *Saturn) and to the corresponding type of metal (gold, silver, iron, mercury, tin, copper, lead). The seven different capitals of the columns were echoed in the shape of two-dimensional emblems (seals) arranged round a seven-pointed star. The same sequence was also represented in relief in seven different types of metal. These seals, likewise designed by Rudolf Steiner, can be regarded as pictorial or sculptural representations of the types of spiritual influence the planets exert on the *earth.

Rudolf Steiner: *The Spiritual Hierarchies and the Physical World*, GA 110.

Planetary sphere — the entire sphere of influence of a planet in our solar system. This influence reaches far beyond the actual planet itself and is enclosed by the orbit it makes round the *sun. In the Ptolemaic system, with the *earth at the centre, the *moon and the *sun are also regarded as planets, thus giving seven planets: Sun, Moon, Mars, Mercury, Jupiter, Venus, Saturn. This view dates from the days in which the moving lights in the sky, in contrast to the fixed stars, were called 'wanderers' (planets). The influence of a planet can be studied in *minerals, *plants, *animals and *humankind. The rotation of the earth rhythmically exposes its creatures to cosmic influences from all regions of the universe. Although Uranus, Neptune and Pluto also exert an influence, they are not included in this ancient system. According to Rudolf *Steiner, these three planets were attracted into the solar system after it had already developed into its present form.

Rudolf Steiner: *The Spiritual Hierarchies and the Physical World*, GA 110.

Planetary stages — successive stages of our solar system's past evolution are known as: Ancient Saturn, Ancient Sun, Ancient Moon, Earth. During this last stage the present planet *earth developed. The *first* phase of Earth development (a capital E distinguishes the stage from the actual planet) is called *Polaris, when, following 'pralaya' (or the spiritual interlude after Old Moon), the solar system was still a homogeneous unity. At the end of this stage the present planet Saturn appeared as an independent planet. The *second* phase is called *Hyperborea, during which further condensation from spirit to physical substances took place, and the present Jupiter, Mars, Venus and Mercury were formed. The *third* stage is called *Lemuria, during which the present moon was expelled from the earth and formed a separate celestial body. The Pacific Basin may be regarded as the scar left in planet earth after the moon departed. Lemuria was followed by the *fourth* stage,

94

called *Atlantis. After the disappearance of Atlantis due to an enormous flood, the post-Atlantean *cultural periods developed until our present day. The current stage of Earth will develop into three further stages or planetary embodiments, called *Jupiter, *Venus, *Vulcan — each stage separated by an intervening 'pralaya'.

From Rudolf *Steiner's description of the evolutionary stages of our solar system, it appears that *mankind has participated in this evolution from the beginning. Man and cosmos form a unity. From the outset through to the very last stage, mankind will have experienced a huge transformative process — from a human germ on Ancient *Saturn to an angelic being, called the tenth *hierarchy, on future *Vulcan.

Rudolf Steiner: *Occult Science*, GA 13.

Planetary symbols — see: Christmas tree.

Planetary types — also called: 'soul types'. Between two *incarnations, the *'I' lives in the spiritual world where it travels through the following sequence of *planetary spheres: *Moon, Mercury, *Venus, *Sun, Mars, *Jupiter, *Saturn. When the 'I' is again born on *earth, it arrives there with all the knowledge it has been able to absorb during its sojourn in the spiritual world. This newly acquired knowledge manifests in the *soul of the new human being. However, the planetary sphere where the 'I' stayed longest, and where it was able to really absorb new spiritual knowledge, will leave a predominant imprint on the soul. This imprint becomes more visible when the *astral body emancipates itself from life processes, and is 'born' as an independent member around the age of 14. This imprint affects our general psychological make-up.

Rudolf Steiner: *Karmic Relationships, Vol. 2*, lecture 10, GA 236; Max Stibbe: *Seven Soul Types*.

Plant — see: Mankind.

Polaris

Polaris — see: Planetary stages.

Post-Atlantean period — see: Cultural periods.

Pre-existence — in a broad sense, the period between two lives in which the *'I', after having gradually cast off the preceding life, is guided and inspired by the *hierarchies to start creating new conditions for its next incarnation on *earth. In a narrower sense, it is the period just prior to a new birth. Rudolf *Steiner suggested the term 'unbornhood' (*Ungeborenheit*) as a counterpart to 'mortality', so as to encompass the whole human experience both on earth and in the world of spirit. In the background of the *Sistine Madonna* by Raphael (1483–1520), one can see many heads of children on their way to being born on *earth. The painting is frequently hung in Waldorf kindergartens.

Rudolf Steiner: *Spiritual Hierarchies and the Physical World*, GA 110; *Study of Man*, GA 293; Peter Selg: *Unbornness. Human Pre-Existence and the Journey Towards Birth*.

Preparations — in his Agricultural Course in 1924, Rudolf *Steiner told his audience about preparations that could enhance the vitality of the soil, compost and plants. In *biodynamic agriculture and horticulture, these preparations are still applied and often prepared on site. The preparations, frequently combining an animal with a plant substance — such as a cow horn filled with cow manure and placed in the earth over winter to absorb cosmic forces — enable the plants to better absorb all necessary cosmic influences, thus enhancing nutritional value. By this means, plants are also better protected against all kinds of damaging influences. In recent years, additional biodynamic preparations have been developed for use in areas where the environment is polluted, and the traditional preparations do not have a sufficient vitality-enhancing effect. Recently a new generation of wine growers, some of whom do not otherwise espouse anthroposophy, have been using biodynamic preparations and methods to great effect.

Rudolf Steiner: *Agricultural Course*, GA 327.

Pure thinking — active thinking, in which the thinker becomes conscious of his own will-imbued power of thought. This is in contrast to thinking as passive registering of the inner or outer world. Here, thoughts seem to emerge from phenomena around us and pass into the soul more or less unconsciously, largely occupying our minds and determining how we behave. In pure thinking, however, the higher *'I' is aware of the thinking process and, in addition to this, all subconscious influences from the *physical body, the *ether body and the *astral body are kept at bay. Awareness of the 'I' as consisting of two aspects, the lower and the higher 'I', can help develop this kind of thinking.

Rudolf Steiner: *Study of Man*, GA 293; *The Boundaries of Natural Science*, GA 322; *The Philosophy of Freedom*, GA 4.

R

Rainbow — according to the story in the Bible (Genesis 9: 12–17), God gave the rainbow after the Flood as a sign of his covenant with Noah, promising never to let anything similar happen again. Before the Flood, the atmosphere of the *earth was apparently so dense that a phenomenon like the rainbow could not occur. After the Flood, atmospheric circumstances had fundamentally changed. The period before the Flood is dealt with extensively by Rudolf Steiner in his accounts of *Atlantis. Due to their natural *clairvoyance, the Atlanteans had no difficulties in finding their way through the misty atmosphere of Atlantis. After the Flood, humankind slowly adapted to the new environment and, according to the Edda, thought of the rainbow as a bridge to the spiritual world.

Rudolf Steiner: *Cosmic Memory*, GA 11.

Reincarnation — *anthroposophy teaches that the *'I' experiences various lives on *earth. The immortal 'I' alternately lives in the spiritual world and in the physical world. In both worlds human development continues. When someone is born again, he has a new opportunity to complete tasks left uncompleted in a previous life. In the spiritual world between two *incarnations, the 'I' has the opportunity to absorb spiritual information instilled by the *hierarchies. The extent to which it will be able to absorb this spiritual wisdom depends on experiences and perceptions gained in the previous life on earth. Rudolf Steiner saw it as his task to reintroduce the age-old concept of reincarnation and *karma to the western world. The concept of reincarnation sheds a consolatory and clarifying light on humanity's purpose on earth.

Rudolf Steiner: *Manifestations of Karma*, GA 120; *Reincarnation and Karma*, GA 135.

Religious education — in response to a question in 1919 from parents of the first *Waldorf school in Stuttgart, Germany, Rudolf *Steiner introduced religious education as a separate subject of the Waldorf curriculum. This type of religious education, given by specially trained teachers, is not linked to a certain system of belief, but is intended to present pupils with an open attitude towards all kinds of religious views. It aims first and foremost to awaken the child's natural reverence for the marvel and beauty of life. In addition to this type of religious education, at some Waldorf schools religious studies are offered at parents' request, by teachers from different religious denominations who visit the school once a week. Thus, children of all religious backgrounds, or none, can attend Waldorf schools.

In general it can be said that Waldorf schools, though not subscribing to beliefs of a particular denomination, tend to be spiritually oriented to a generally Christian perspective. The seasonal *festivals celebrated in the schools are drawn from the Christian tradition. Waldorf schools located in other than traditionally Christian cultures also celebrate festivals derived from local religious traditions.

In response to another question, Rudolf Steiner inaugurated religious services for students outside the Waldorf curriculum. These services usually take place on Sundays.

Rudolf Steiner: *Spiritual Ground of Education*, GA 305.

Representative of Humanity, The — sculpture, nine-and-a-half metres high made of elmwood by Rudolf *Steiner and the English sculptress Edith Maryon. It depicts *Christ as embodied love standing at the point of equilibrium between

Representative of Humanity, The

*Lucifer and *Ahriman, and keeping these contrary powers in balance. It was intended to stand in the first *Goetheanum, which burnt down before the sculpture was finished. It now stands in the second *Goetheanum in *Dornach, Switzerland.

Rudolf Steiner: *World History in the Light of Anthroposophy*, GA 233.

Resurrection — following the Crucifixion on Golgotha, *Christ resurrected from the dead after three days. This event is commemorated in the Christian religion at *Easter. Since his resurrection, Christ has been perceptible to the schooled eye in the *etheric aura of the *earth. Through his deed on Golgotha, the four kingdoms of nature were entirely reinvigorated. Without Christ's deed, and the renewal it caused, the earth would have declined in vitality, and humankind would increasingly have fallen prey to matter.

Rudolf Steiner: *From Jesus to Christ*, GA 131.

Review — (German: *Rückschau*). *Meditation exercise in which, at the end of each day, the whole sequence of that day's events is reviewed in reverse order back to the moment of waking up in the morning. Thus time's normal, logical progression is reversed. The inner effort required for carrying out this meditation causes a loosening of the *'I' from the *physical body, resulting in inner peace and relaxation as a prelude to falling asleep. At the same time, the exercise teaches us how to gain a more objective and serene view of all the day's events, by seeing ourselves from without. It also prepares for a better understanding of the spiritual world in sleep and after death, when the flow of time runs backwards relative to earthly conditions. See also: Supplementary exercises.

Rudolf Steiner: *Secrets of the Threshold*, GA 147; *The Riddle of Humanity*, GA 170; Martina Maria Sam (ed.): *Strengthening the Will, The Review Exercises* (various GAs).

Rhythm — in the anthroposophical image of the human being, rhythm plays an important role as the indefatigable bearer of life — which we can feel for instance when dancing. In rhythmic activity, the body seems to withdraw from gravity, and we are less bound by physical weight. When the music stops, awareness of gravity reasserts itself. This phenomenon is caused by the activity of the *astral body, which is extremely sensitive to music. Like the strings of a puppet, the astral body lifts our *physical body out of gravity as soon as music resounds. Soldiers know that marching to music, likewise, considerably lightens their efforts.

Rhythm can also be seen in the tidal movements of the sea, in the alternation of day and night, in sleeping and waking up, and in the seasons. In the physical body, rhythm is embodied in the inexhaustible workings of the heart and the lungs. In the threefold image of the human being as head-trunk-abdomen, breathing in and breathing out balances the influences of the head and of the metabolic system. This tripartite physical division is reflected in the psychological faculties of *thinking, *feeling and *will, where thinking and will are kept in balance by the mediating pole of feeling. Teachers notice that lessons providing a good alternation of thinking and will activity are often most effective. In ancient Greece, people identified the thinking pole as belonging to the god *Apollo, and the will pole to the god *Dionysus. If one of these two gains the upper hand, we fall out of balance. It is the rhythmic system which ensures that equilibrium is, as far as possible, maintained.

Rudolf Steiner: *Study of Man*, GA 293.

Rite — a series of religious acts or rituals intended to draw the supersensible into the sensible world. *Anthroposophy can facilitate a sense of rite or worship in which the spirit in the human being is guided to the spirit in the universe. This process is described by Rudolf *Steiner in the first of his *Leading Thoughts* (GA 26). The *Christmas Foundation Meeting in Dornach in 1923 may be regarded as a rite in which anthroposophy descended from the spiritual world and was united with life on *earth.

Rudolf Steiner: *The Christmas Conference*, GA 260; *Anthroposophical Leading Thoughts*, GA 26; Sergei O. Prokofieff: *Rudolf Steiner and the Founding of the New Mysteries.*

Rosencreutz, Christian (Germany, 1378–1484) — inspired what was later called 'Rosicrucianism'. Rudolf *Steiner calls him a spiritual leader of mankind who is continually incarnated and active on *earth. His leadership is linked to the impulse of the Count of St Germain in the second half of the eighteenth century, which inspired social and spiritual change under the motto of 'Liberty, Equality, Fraternity'. Unfortunately, the whole enterprise shattered during the violent French Revolution that started in 1789.

Many age-old *fairy-tales, such as those collected by the Grimm brothers, can be regarded as inspired by the same Rosicrucian impulse. *The Fairy-Tale of the Green Snake and the Beautiful Lily* by *Goethe (1749–1832) drew on the same source. The figure of the Man with the Lamp in that story says: 'The time has come!' Rudolf Steiner tells us that the tale represents events in the spiritual world at that period, in the 'School of *Michael'. The time had come when secret *esoteric wisdom should be revealed on earth. In this sense, Goethe's fairy-tale is a precursor of *anthroposophy, a *spiritual science in which Rosicrucian inspiration has assumed contemporary form.

Rudolf Steiner: *Rosicrucian Wisdom*, GA 99.

Rosicrucian stream — one of the four *Mystery streams that underpin *anthroposophy. The mythical *initiate Hermes Trismegistus, the founder of ancient Egypt, is seen as the one who gave the original impulse for this Mystery stream, which Christian *Rosencreutz eventually brought to northern Europe. At the start of the seventeenth century his followers, the Rosicrucians, tried to introduce new inspiration in Europe, for instance through publication of the booklet *The Chymical Wedding of Christian Rosencreutz* (1616). This impulse was nipped in the bud and the impulse went underground. Social impulses prior to the French Revolution can also be seen as an attempt by the same stream to instil a new sense of spirituality, but unfortunately this failed. Rudolf *Steiner reintroduced the *esoteric Rosicrucian stream in his *anthroposophy.

Rudolf Steiner: *Original Impulses for the Science of the Spirit*, GA 96; Frances Yates: *The Rosicrucian Enlightenment*.

Rosy Cross — also Rose Cross. Symbol associated with Christian *Rosencreutz. In *anthroposophy it refers to an image used during meditation in which a black cross is pictured inwardly with a circle of seven red roses, growing from the black wood at the intersection of the two beams. The cross represents our conquered *instincts, drives and *desires. The seven roses represent the purified human *members.

Rudolf Steiner: *Occult Science*, GA 13; *The Stages of Higher Knowledge*, GA 12; Jörgen Smit: *Meditation, Guiding Our Lives for the Encounter with Christ*.

S

St John's — the *festival on 24 June in honour of St John the Baptist (John 1: 29–34). In *Waldorf schools, this festival is sometimes celebrated in the open air with a big bonfire, refreshments, music and dancing. At the end, pupils of the higher classes, often the ones about to leave school, are allowed to jump over the fire. A St John's story is often told as well.

Rudolf *Steiner outlines how, around midsummer, the *earth has breathed out all her *elemental beings. The earth at this time is in a state of *sleep, and the whole of nature has grown out into the visible world in the shape of leaves and flowers. Christian and pagan elements blend in this age-old festival. In his saying, 'I must decrease, but he must increase', the figure of John, who prepared the way for Christ's coming, simultaneously embodies the moment when the outer power of the sun and physical life start to wane, and heralds the change of consciousness and growth of inner spirit required in humanity's further evolution.

Rudolf Steiner: *The Festivals and Their Meaning.*

St Martin — festival on 11 November in honour of St Martin who, according to the legend, cut his cloak in half to give one part to a beggar, who afterwards turned out to be *Christ.

In many *Waldorf schools this festival involves making lanterns out of turnips, carrots, pumpkins, or cardboard and transparent paper. Then, on 11 November, when darkness has fallen, the children go out into the street or a park, processing with their lanterns and singing St Martin songs. The light in the lantern symbolizes the fact that in the dark season the light of the summer sun has gradually descended into the *earth and then, through *Advent, is born again within. As *Jesus is born at *Christmas, this inner light shines out from each individual. The bright lanterns in the gathering darkness of late autumn herald the beginning of this process.

Rudolf Steiner: *The Festivals and Their Meaning.*

Saints' legends — *fables and saints' legends form the main story material told throughout the school year in Class Two of *Waldorf schools. In the animals depicted in fables, all sorts of human one-sidedness are shown. In the lives of saints, by contrast, the stories are of human beings who have overcome imbalance to achieve self-mastery. Saints can be said to have mastered all lower influences of the *astral body. That is why, in these legends, saints are often depicted surrounded by loving and obedient animals. St Francis is often depicted with birds feeding from his hand, and St Jerome is attended by a lion.

The lives of saints are told to children at about age seven because, at that phase, their own astral body starts to develop a certain independence. For the first time they will be confronted with all the influences inherent in this 'astrality'. Fables and saints' lives can guide these youngsters through this developmental stage and help them find balance between different extremes.

Salamanders — *elemental beings related to the *element of fire.

Sanguine — one of the four *temperaments. The *astral body predominates here, and there is a particular relationship with the *element of air. Sanguine people flutter through life like butterflies, delighting in and continually imbibing new sense impressions. Friendships are easily made and easily ended. There is a preference for bright primary colours, reflected in the choice of clothes and home decor. The danger of this temperament is a tendency to superficiality, or a chaotic approach to things. Sanguine people thrive on variety and frequent change. In general, young children always have a certain sanguine character, since they are so open to fleeting and fluctuating sense impressions.

Rudolf Steiner: *Discussions with Teachers*, GA 295.

Satan — see: Ahriman.

Saturn — see: Planetary stages,

Schröer, Karl Julius — (1825–1900). Rudolf *Steiner's teacher of German language and literature at the Technical High School in Vienna, Austria. Karl Julius Schröer was instrumental in awakening Rudolf Steiner's interest in the works of *Goethe, leading to Rudolf Steiner's work at the Goethe and Schiller Archive in Weimar, Germany, from 1890–1897. As a philologist, Karl Julius Schröer also rediscovered the old *Christmas plays that had been performed for many generations in Oberufer, Austria/Hungary. These plays are now staged every Christmas in *Waldorf schools and in other anthroposophic *fields of work.

Rudolf Steiner: *Autobiography*, GA 28.

Seasons — The *earth breathes like a living being. This process is expressed in the four seasons in northern and southern hemispheres. On the summer side of the planet, the earth breathes out, while on the winter side the planet breathes in. This rhythmical alternation occurs due to the oblique position of the earth's axis. The *elemental world also experiences this seasonal change, expressed in changes and cycles in the plant world. Close observation of this continual change, in which the *hierarchies also play a part, can raise awareness of the life-giving forces on which all life on earth depends. The Christian festivals, often drawing on ancient pagan celebrations, are embedded in the seasonal cycle in a way which gives them added meaning as a cycle of flourishing and waning life, mirrored by an alternation in the human being between greater inwardness and enhanced awareness of outer surroundings, and paralleled by stages in the life and death of *Christ.

Rudolf Steiner: *The Festivals and Their Meaning.*

Senses — there are twelve senses. The lower four are: *touch, *life, *movement, *balance. In normal circumstances we are not consciously aware of these senses, which are also called the *'will' senses. With these senses we get in touch with our own corporality.

The middle senses are: *warmth, *sight, *taste, *smell. Usually we are half-aware of them, and they enable us to interact with the surrounding world. They are also called the *'feeling' senses.

The upper-senses are: *'I'-sense, *thought, *language, *hearing. We are fully aware of these senses, which enable us to communicate with our fellow human beings. They are also called the *'thinking' senses.

Rudolf Steiner: *The World of the Senses and the World of the Spirit*, GA 134; A. Soesman: *Our Twelve Senses.*

Sentient body — the part of the *astral body that enables us to gather sense impressions from, and respond to, the surrounding world. Both animals and human beings have a sentient body. From a historical point of view, it can be said that the human sentient body reached a certain stage of independence during the ancient Persian *cultural period (from 5000 BC onwards). Before this stage human beings were *clairvoyant to such an extent that they did not develop objective perception, with self-detachment. People were too involved in their surroundings for this to be possible, and the sentient body was therefore not yet emancipated but instead actively participated in and responded to all influences. Initiated priests, who had learned objective detachment, taught their pupils how to develop this new way of perceiving the world.

Rudolf Steiner: *Theosophy*, GA 9.

Sentient soul — the part of the *astral body which focuses and sustains our individual consciousness. All sense impressions entering through the *sentient body flow into this individual consciousness. Physical abilities, sight, hearing, etc., determine and limit the range and scope of the sentient soul. From a historical point of view it can be said that the sentient soul reached a certain stage of independence during the ancient Egyptian-Babylonian *cultural period (from 3000 BC onward). In this period human beings learned to objectify the world around them and accordingly *clairvoyance decreased considerably. Both animals and human beings have a sentient soul. The reason for the different quality of the sentient soul in animals, which do not have individual but group consciousness, and humans, is that in us the *'I' is also active and working 'down' upon the astral body.

Rudolf Steiner: *Theosophy*, GA 9.

Seraphim — spiritual beings belonging to the first *hierarchy. Also called 'Spirits of Love'. The Seraphim are the highest members of the first hierarchy, who received the impulse from God to create man and the solar system as an environment in which he could evolve. The Seraphim designed the spiritual idea of the future earth and cosmos.

Rudolf Steiner: *The Spiritual Hierarchies and the Physical World*, GA 110.

Sevenfold image of the human being — at present we consist of seven *members or bodily sheaths, the last three of which are still at a germinal stage of future development. These seven are: *physical body, *ether body, *astral body, *'I', *spirit self, *life spirit and *spirit man. The 'I' occupies an intermediate position between the physical world and the spiritual world, and thus opens up both worlds.

Rudolf Steiner: *Theosophy*, GA 9.

Shaded drawing — drawing technique taught in *Waldorf schools in which the picture is built up by drawing short, slanting lines. A picture thus appears on a sheet of paper not by drawing its outline but by slowly composing the surface of an image. By varying the length and the proximity of the lines, the picture acquires a vibrant character. Patterns of light and shade can easily be built up. Colours can subtly be blended in this way as well. Just presenting the outline of an object in a drawing is an abstract way of representing reality, since outlines in themselves do not exist in nature. In fact, the eye experiences reality as a patchwork of coloured surfaces; and the artist, as well as the beholder, will experience the dynamic process and movement at work in this kind of drawing. This technique can also be seen as a means to trace and portray creative, dynamic forces at work in nature.

Valerie Jacobs: *Black and White Shaded Drawing.*

Sight — see: Eyesight.

Skeleton — the hardest part of the human body. Also, the part in which the forces of death are most apparent. This hardening process is ascribed to the influence of *Ahriman. Careful observation shows that every part of the skeleton consists of three segments. Every bone has a kind of head, a middle part and a 'foot'. This observation has led to the idea that the whole skeleton is informed by a threefold structure. Every bone is a *metamorphosis of this basic pattern. This idea is present in the works of *Goethe (1749–1832) and can also be found in the anthroposophic concept of *mankind, in which the *physical body is seen in part as a metamorphosis of the previous life's physical body, as well as a product of inheritance.

L.F.C. Mees MD: *Secrets of the Skeleton.*

Sleep — absence of consciousness, similar to the lack of awareness in the lower pole of the human being, where metabolic processes take place. The arms and legs also belong to this pole. We are not aware of digestive or metabolic processes except when they are afflicted by some disorder, when we become conscious of them through pain. The movements of our limbs also take place below the threshold of awareness. We know what we want to do with our limbs but we do not consciously experience the process whereby intention passes into movement. When we want to pick up an object from a table, we automatically form our fingers into the corresponding shape and size. When we walk to a certain place, we do not consciously think of our feet. See also: Will.

Sleep also of course refers to the state of lying in bed and losing consciousness altogether. Here the *'I' and the *astral body rise out of the *ether body and the *physical body, which both remain lying in bed. Until we wake up again, the 'I' and the astral body dwell in the world of spirit among the *hierarchies, where they draw new inspiration. The ether body and the physical body are also refreshed during the night by the hierarchies, which sustain them in the absence of the astral body and 'I'. Thus we can start the new day refreshed when the four *members of the human being are reunited. *Dreaming, which is a kind of inter-mediate state of consciousness, mostly occurs as the astral body and 'I' are either departing or returning to their connection with the physical and etheric bodies. *Anthroposophy regards sleep as an important aspect of children's education, when they can work through and more deeply absorb what has been learned, and thus patterns of learning are structured to take full account of this rhythmic occurrence.

Rudolf Steiner: *A Psychology of Body, Soul and Spirit*, GA 115; Audrey MacAllen: *Sleep*.

Smell — one of the 12 *senses. Through this sense the outer world enters human awareness in a subtle but insistent way, since we are unable to shut ourselves off from odours. Essential properties of the outer world that remain imperceptible to other senses are revealed through this sense. We immediately discern whether a scent impression is pleasant or unpleasant, and thus this sense functions as a warning system.

Rudolf Steiner: *Study of Man*, GA 293; Albert Soesman: *Our Twelve Senses*.

Social science — see: Social threefolding.

Social therapy — developed from *curative education and inspired by Karl König (1902–1966), the founder of the Camphill Movement, which started in Scotland in 1939. In small communities, such as farms, people with developmental difficulties can work, learn and live together in a mutually supportive environment. Disabilities are not treated as illnesses, but as part of each individual's overall spectrum of potential. Specially trained social therapists give support and structure to daily life in these communities. Residents engage in all sorts of work — often craftwork and horticulture — and social gatherings, festivals and cultural activities form an essential part of community life. Camphill communities are founded on a sense that every individual is valuable and has something to contribute, and that impairments in one incarnation may be a way to acquire strength for a succeeding one.

Anthroposophic social therapy has spread throughout the globe. There are over 100 Camphill communities — as well as many other non-Camphill but anthroposophically-based communities for people with special needs — in the world.

Rudolf Steiner: *Education for Special Needs*, GA 317; Karl König: *Becoming Human: A Social Task*.

Social threefolding — a concept introduced by Rudolf

Social threefolding

*Steiner in 1919. Rather than being an attempt to devise an artificially imposed social programme, it sets out to establish actual laws that work in society, and to clarify and enhance these. Threefold society consists of three, clearly delineated and autonomous realms: spiritual and cultural life, the proper domain of liberty; political life, where equality should rightfully prevail; and economic life where principles of fraternity should be upheld. Whereas the slogan of the French Revolution — 'Liberty, equality, fraternity' — sought to apply these principles in a general way to all society, Steiner regards each principle as having its different and specific sphere of application. Rudolf Steiner's fundamental social law states: *The well-being of a community of people working together will be the greater, the less the individual claims for himself the proceeds of his work. In other words, the more of these proceeds he makes over to his fellow workers, the more his own needs are satisfied, not out of his own work but out of the work done by others.* His suggestions, which he hoped at the time would have real impact on social thinking, largely fell on deaf ears. However, the principles he delineated are ones which remain valid as a diagnostic tool, at least, of where society goes wrong — for example, the way in which cultural and spiritual endeavours are frequently constrained or distorted by financial issues. One might think here of the common lack of independence of scientists engaged in medical research controlled by large commercial corporations, which have a financial interest in the research results. Rudolf Steiner: *Towards Social Renewal*, GA 23; *World Economy*, GA 340.

Soul — in the threefold image of the human being composed of *physical body, soul and *spirit, the term 'soul' refers to the part of the *human being where all sense impressions, feelings and subjective thoughts are inscribed. For example, we see a flower and say, 'How beautiful', responding to it with our soul. If we take this initial response further, we can go on to study the laws at work in the plant, forming ideas and concepts about it — and then we enter the realm of spirit. Characteristic of the world of the soul is that our personal opinion plays a role, whereas the spirit is characterized by absence of personal bias. The soul is a complex of sympathies and antipathies, whereas the world of the spirit is informed by laws that always hold true, irrespective of our opinion: a circle is a circle, whether we like it or not. However, it is possible, and according to Steiner most necessary, to imbue the objective, spiritual faculty of thinking with personal warmth of soul, thus both enlivening otherwise abstract concepts, and rendering so-called subjectivity a more accurate tool of perception.

The soul, like the physical body, only exists while we are incarnated on *earth. It can be further subdivided into *sentient soul, intellectual soul and *consciousness soul, which represent successive evolutionary phases in the soul's development from reactive feeling to more self-governed and self-aware consciousness. All these stages are retained in us like different strata.

As in general usage, the term 'soul' sometimes refers to a human being as a whole, for instance in the phrase 'an old soul', referring to somebody who has had many incarnations on *earth.

Rudolf Steiner: *Theosophy*, GA 9.

Sound ether — see: Ether.

Speech formation — an art of speech and recitation developed by Marie Steiner-von Sivers and Rudolf *Steiner. It aspires to a deeper awareness of the powers inherent in language and speech, aiming to bring these formative powers, and the beings at work in them, to listener's awareness. Speech formed in this way also has healing potency. Attention is paid to the intrinsic nature of the different speech sounds and to breathing, articulation, rhythm, metre, poetry, drama and vocal gesture. Speech formation is used as an accompaniment to *eurythmy and in education, and specially trained speech therapists use it in a therapeutic context.

Rudolf Steiner and Marie Steiner-von Sivers: *Creative Speech*, GA 280.

Spirit — in general referring to the immaterial world, which is the source of the physical world. In human beings, the spirit is embodied in the fourth member, the *'I'. Although living in a physical body on *earth, the 'I' belongs to the spiritual world, and thus serves as a link between the physical and spiritual world. Anthroposophic exercises and meditations are focused on developing our conscious 'I'-based connection with the spiritual world. Spirit, as distinct from *soul, is objective and holds sway in all phenomena and beings: a realm to which human subjectivity can gradually elevate itself. See also: Soul.

Rudolf Steiner: *Anthroposophical Leading Thoughts*, GA 26.

Spirit man — during life on *earth, the *'I' lives in the three human *members: *physical body, *ether body and *astral body. During a lifelong process of mutual influence between these three members and the 'I', the 'I' slowly appropriates parts of them. The last, and most difficult, member to undergo this 'I'-transformation is the physical body, resulting in what is called 'spirit man'. Unlike the physical body itself, its transformed aspect as 'spirit man' does not disappear after death, but is taken by the 'I' into the next *incarnation, where this transformational process continues. We can regard the aim of life on earth as being to slowly transform all the bodily sheaths so as to give rise to a completely spiritualized human being.

Rudolf Steiner: *Theosophy*, GA 9.

Spirit self — the part of the astral body which is transformed by the *'I' during life on *earth (see also: Spirit man). We can regard this as the humanized and purified part of the astral body. The 'spirit self' does not disappear after death, but is taken by the 'I' into the next incarnation, where this transformational process continues. We can regard the aim of life on earth as being to slowly transform all the bodily sheaths so as to give rise to a completely spiritualized human being.

Rudolf Steiner: *Theosophy*, GA 9.

Spirits of the Age — see: Archai.

Spiritual science — translation of the German term *Geisteswissenschaft*. In using this term, Rudolf Steiner tried to unite mainstream science with spiritual insights gained in a rigorous, disciplined — and thus scientific — way through developing and applying *clairvoyant capacities and supersensible perception. The terms 'spiritual science' and 'anthroposophy' are interchangeable in this context.

Steiner, Rudolf — born in Kraljevec, in modern-day Croatia, on 27 February 1861, died in *Dornach, Switzerland, on 30 March 1925. Founder of the *spiritual science which he called *anthroposophy. He trained his *clairvoyant faculties to enable him to undertake research into spiritual realities, reintroducing the concepts of *karma and *reincarnation into the Western world and advocating methods whereby modern human beings can reconnect with the *spirit in the cosmos. He gave about 6000 lectures throughout Europe, the greater part of which were recorded in shorthand. These lectures, together with his books and his many other publications, have been translated into many languages. His seminal ideas have given birth to various anthroposophic *fields of work. Despite his extraordinary insights into an astonishing range of different fields — ranging, for example, from architecture to agriculture, from medicine to meditation, from education

Steiner, Rudolf

to science, and from history to poetry — he had no desire to be hailed as a guru, but wished those inspired by him to form their own ideas and reach their own conclusions.

Rudolf Steiner: *Autobiography*, GA 28; Henk van Oort: *Anthroposophy, A Concise Introduction.*

Steiner schools — see Waldorf.

Sun — physical abode of the sun spirit, who has been given different names in various cultural epochs, such as *Ahura Mazda, Amun Ra and *Christ. These all refer to the same spirit who has always been connected with the *earth, and who eventually incarnated in the body of *Jesus. There are references to the same sun spirit in the sun worship of Ancient Celtic and Germanic tribes. *Anthroposophy casts new light on these cultural concepts. Kings and emperors identified with this spirit when they titled themselves Sol Invictus (Ancient Rome), Le Roi Soleil (France), or stated that they ruled by 'divine right'.

The concept 'Ancient Sun' refers to a *planetary stage prior to our present solar system, during which all planets were still united within an all-embracing cosmic body.

Rudolf Steiner: *Occult Science*, GA 13; Georg Blattmann: *The Sun, The Ancient Mysteries and a New Physics.*

Sun at midnight — at night, when the sun has disappeared behind the *earth, an *initiate can dispel the darkness of matter through his powers of inner vision, to perceive the sun's radiance. Not only the sun can be perceived by this means but also *Christ and other spiritual beings who dwell in the sun. This capacity is called 'seeing the sun at midnight'. With the same purpose, priests of ancient cultures entered inner chambers or dark temples to practise inner vision. See also: Initiation; Midnight hour.

Rudolf Steiner: *The Festivals and Their Meaning*; *Karmic Relationships Vol. 2*, GA 236.

Supplementary exercises — six basic exercises for spiritual

116

development, given by Rudolf *Steiner on various occasions. They are: mastery of *thinking, through concentration; mastery of *will impulses, through actions not imposed by any outward necessity; mastery of *feelings by developing equanimity; positivity, by seeking positive aspects in even the most negative of occurrences; open-mindedness, by practising willingness to contemplate the possibility of things we might otherwise dismiss as untrue; harmony, by combining all five previous exercises in overall equilibrium.

These six exercises, as preparation and foundation for other forms of meditation, were regarded as vital by Steiner for ensuring we stay in balance and close to life's realities when engaging in meditative work. See also: Meditation.

Rudolf Steiner: *Knowledge of the Higher Worlds*, GA 10; *Occult Science*, GA 13; *Stages of Higher Knowledge*, GA 12. *Guidance in Esoteric Training*, GA 245; Ates Baydur (ed.): *Six Steps in Self-Development*.

Sylphs — air spirits. See: Elemental beings.

Sympathy — the quality of *soul whereby we merge with the world around us. This quality has its physical location in the warmth of our blood. In the sequence *thinking, *feeling and *will, sympathy is oriented to the will. Its opposite is *antipathy, which is related to the colder pole of head-focused thinking. Neither antipathy nor sympathy are regarded as positive or negative in themselves, but are deemed to be necessary fluctuations of soul life through which we can both connect with the world and detach ourselves from it.

Rudolf Steiner: *Study of Man*, GA 293.

T

Tadpole — referring to the human figure in children's drawings until about the age of three, consisting of just the head with arms and legs attached to it. The trunk is missing. This representation of the human form occurs universally at this age. In these drawings the lower pole, the seat of *will, is attached to the upper pole, the head. The pole between, of *feeling, is not yet present. Thus we can see that young children are as yet in a state of relative sleep, immersed in the lower pole, where digestive forces reign. This exactly represents the stage in which the infant finds himself. Powers of thought, characterized by awareness and alertness, still await development. As soon as the child awakens a little more, the trunk separating the head from the metabolic system will appear in drawings. To parents and teachers, this knowledge is of great value because it reveals a stage of, as yet, sleep-like development which should not be roused prematurely. Trying to teach children at this age to engage in more head-focused activities, such as learning to read, can injure the life forces which this state of *sleep is absorbed in developing.
Rudolf Steiner: *Study of Man*, GA 293.

Taste — through this *sense the outer world enters and penetrates us. Just looking at an unknown food, for instance, will tell us much less than tasting it. After tasting we can decide to eat more, or not. Thus taste is a guardian of our physical health. The sense of *smell works quite similarly but taste takes the probing process a step further by dissolving part of the food in our mouth and thus allowing it access to our body.
Rudolf Steiner: *Study of Man*, GA 293; Albert Soesman: *Our Twelve Senses*.

Temperament — the four temperaments are: *choleric, *phlegmatic, *sanguine, *melancholic. Each of the four temperaments is determined more by one of the four human *members, the *physical body, *ether body, *astral body or *'I'. The prevailing member will cause the corresponding temperament to come to the fore. It is common for one temperament to predominate, but for two others to be present as well, and for one to be more or less lacking (for instance, a primarily choleric person might have subtler melancholic and sanguine traits, but next to nothing of the phlegmatic temperament). In general, it can be said that if the physical body exerts a relatively strong influence upon the personality, the melancholic temperament will appear. A prevailing ether body causes the phlegmatic temperament. If the astral body is strongest, the sanguine temperament will arise. If the 'I' prevails, this leads to a choleric temperament.

Knowledge of the temperaments can be very helpful in education. Behaviour becomes much more understandable once we regard temperament as a kind of cloak the child is wearing. The child's prevailing temperament is not the child himself, but is an influence and attribute of a dominant bodily sheath. Each temperament also responds best to particular approaches and forms of teaching. A choleric child, for instance, likes to be challenged (but never to be seen to have failed) whereas the same degree of challenge may make a melancholic feel hopeless. A sanguine child loves a succession of different themes, whereas the phlegmatic child will still be thinking about the first thing when everyone has moved on to the next.

In adult life we can try to balance our own predominant temperament. Although not an easy task, the qualities of the other temperaments can be developed to try to harmonize the way we respond to the world. Temperament is

Temperament

determined both by tendencies that developed in previous lives and genetic factors in the present life.

Rudolf Steiner: *The Four Temperaments*, GA 57; *Discussions with Teachers*, GA 295.

Theosophy — literally: divine wisdom. The Theosophical Society was founded in New York in 1875 by Helena P. Blavatsky (1831–1891) and others. The term is also the title of a book by Rudolf *Steiner published in 1904, when he was a member of the Theosophical Society. Later, following disagreement about fundamental principles, instigated by claims which Rudolf Steiner disputed, that the young Krishnamurti was a reincarnation of *Christ, Steiner and many in the German section of the Theosophical Society left to form the Anthroposophical Society. The book entitled *Theosophy* thus deals with spiritual content that would later be called anthroposophy.

Rudolf Steiner: *Theosophy*, GA 9.

Thinking — faculty of the brain acting as a mirror to reflect thoughts. The brain does not produce thought. The non-physical, dynamic thinking patterns originating in the *spirit are reflected in the brain in concepts and definitions. The *'I' enacts this process, with the help of the beings of the third *hierarchy, and the *soul force of antipathy allows it to come to awareness in us through detachment from our surroundings. Thinking is a *metamorphosis of *will activity, which is restrained in order to give rise to thought. A dog cannot really think because it is immersed in physical movement, 'wagging out' all thoughts with its tail rather than being detached from them enough to think. In other words, in thinking, movement must come to a standstill; and young children only slowly learn to master this process once they awaken more from sleep-like or vegetative conditions of bodily growth. While growing up, human beings learn how to reject or regulate impulses through the power

120

of thought. This is an important consideration in *Waldorf education, especially with regard to the early developmental sequence of walking-talking-thinking. Each earlier stage provides an essential foundation for the next, and *will activity and movement are vital as a basis for sound thinking to later develop. When new concepts are to be taught, the Waldorf teacher preferably starts with the *will and then works from there *upwards* to the head, where the brain can mirror the movements of the limbs. Multiplication tables can be walked, clapped or stamped, for instance. Numeracy skills are practised in a most active way, and in the mirroring brain all movements will eventually come to a standstill in well-delineated concepts. The same approach is used in foreign language teaching. Finger games and movement songs first engage the *will, and gradually the new language comes to be reflected conceptually in the brain. See also: Imitation.

Rudolf Steiner: *Study of Man*, GA 293; *The Philosophy of Freedom*, GA 4.

Thought, sense of — one of the 12 *senses. Also called: Concept sense. With this sense we can understand the message clothed in language by looking not only beyond the sound but also the language itself. In this way the message is freed from the language. We can 'look through' the sound 'chien', 'Hund', 'hond', 'dog', or 'canis' to arrive at the soundless concept which all languages point at in their different ways. This does not, of course, mean that the qualitative differences between languages are unimportant, only that above and beyond these differences a uniting archetypal concept can be found.

Rudolf Steiner: *Study of Man*, GA 293; Albert Soesman: *Our Twelve Senses*.

Threefold human being — refers to the three aspects of *body, *soul and *spirit. See also: Dichotomy and Trichotomy.

Threshold

Threshold — in general: the boundary between the physical and the supersensible worlds. We can pass beyond this threshold in earthly life through the kind of training that *anthroposophy can offer, as well as passing it inevitably at death. Rudolf *Steiner informs us about two *guardians at this threshold. We can only consciously cross the threshold to the world of spirit by becoming fully conscious, self-aware and autonomous beings, who not only understand our own task in life but also the broader aims of all Creation.

Rudolf Steiner: *The Threshold of the Spiritual World*, GA 17.

Thrones — spiritual beings belonging to the first *hierarchy. Also called 'Spirits of Will'. They realized the impulse of *God to create man and the solar system. The Thrones provided the initial substance out of which the material world has evolved.

Rudolf Steiner: *The Spiritual Hierarchies and the Physical World*, GA 110; *Occult Science*, GA 13.

Touch, sense of — one of the 12 *senses. This sense acquaints us with the boundaries of our own *physical body. Every touch experience anchors the *'I' within the physical body, at the same time helping us to delineate and demarcate ourselves from the surrounding world. If we could not literally get in touch with the physical world, we would live in a dream state without self-awareness. By coming up against the physical world, and connecting with it through touch, or by bumping into things accidentally, falling and getting up again, a child not only learns about the physical world but also becomes acquainted with his own body.

Albert Soesman: *Our Twelve Senses*.

Trichotomy — division into three parts. In the anthroposophic context this refers to the *threefold human being of *body, *soul and *spirit, in contrast with prevalent Western views, which we can trace back to Descartes, of

the human being as duality of body and soul or mind. See
also: Dichotomy.

Trinity — *Father, Son, *Holy Spirit. The cosmos as we know
it today originates in a deed of the Holy Trinity. The actual
task of creation was carried out by the *hierarchies. The
concept of the *Father is associated with the created physical world originating in the past The concept of the Son is
associated with all things in progress, the 'here and now',
and with the deed of *Christ in descending to and
redeeming the *earth. The concept of the *Holy Spirit is
associated with the future of the earth and *mankind. In the
Jordan Baptism, as described in the Bible, we have a picture uniting these three principles: the dove of the Holy
Spirit descending on the human being Jesus, who will
henceforth bear the Christ, and the voice of the Father
resounding from the heavens. The three concepts refer to
aspects of one spiritual and natural divine being who is the
foundation of all life. See also: Whitsun.

Rudolf Steiner: *The Spiritual Hierarchies and the Physical World*, GA
110.

U

Undine — *elemental beings inhabiting or closely related to water.

Rudolf Steiner: *Harmony of the Creative Word*, GA 230.

Urge — aspect of the *will originating from the *ether body.

Rudolf Steiner: *Study of Man*, GA 293.

V

Veil painting — *painting technique applied in *fields of work inspired by *anthroposophy, such as *Waldorf schools. In this technique, watercolours are applied in one thin layer at a time. After the first layer has dried, the second is applied, and so on. In the end, the painting consists of as many fine layers as the painter wishes. This method gives a surprisingly transparent or translucent and shimmering effect. The colours seem to loosen themselves from the actual paint. Looking at such a work of art has a therapeutic effect, as attention is led away from earthly substance and drawn to the dynamic formative forces at work behind the visible world.
Rudolf Steiner: *Colour*, GA 291.

Venus — see: Planetary stages.

Verses — Rudolf *Steiner gave many verses and *meditations which embody the insights of anthroposophy. These verses relate to a huge range of themes including the *festivals, seasons, times of day, birth and death; or are intended for specific purposes such as healing and sustaining courage in difficult times. Often they are what are known as 'mantric verses': this means that the sounds composing them directly invoke the qualities they refer to. In *The Calendar of the Soul* a verse is given for every week of the year. Often Steiner gave a special verse to a particular person, composed with this person in mind. There are also verses spoken by pupils of *Waldorf schools at the beginning of each school day. The most extensive verse by Steiner is the *Foundation Stone Meditation which is fundamental to *anthroposophy.
Rudolf Steiner: *Verses and Meditations* (various GAs); *The Calendar of the Soul*, GA 40; *Meditations* series (various GAs).

Vidar stream — one of the four *mystery streams upon which

Vidar stream

*anthroposophy is founded. The Vidar stream originated in northern Europe and was embodied in the pantheon of Ancient Germanic gods such as Wotan (= Odin), Thor, Freya, Loki and many others. These gods and their acts are described in the Icelandic poem, *The Edda*. Vidar, Odin's son, is a silent god. He survives the Twilight of the Gods — which represents loss of human *clairvoyance, resulting in the fading of contact with the divine world. Vidar eventually conquers the *ahrimanic Fenris wolf, in a story which closely parallels that of the *Archangel *Michael in conquering the dragon. When Michael became the *spirit of the age in 1879, a new type of supersensible perception became possible, as elaborated by anthroposophy.

B.C. Lievegoed: *Mystery Streams in Europe and the New Mysteries.*

Vulcan — see: Planetary stages.

W

Waldorf — in the early twentieth century, Emil Molt, director of the Waldorf-Astoria cigarette factory in Stuttgart, Germany, asked Rudolf *Steiner to help him set up a school for the children of his employees. The first Waldorf school opened its doors in 1919. Rudolf Steiner's approach to the education of children and Emil Molt's commercial ideas united in the founding of the school, which was eventually to lead to many other Waldorf schools throughout the world. By choosing the name of Waldorf, a link was established with other successful enterprises — such as the Waldorf-Astoria Hotel in New York, USA — initiated by the same Astor family, which originated in the village of Waldorf, near Heidelberg, Germany.

Waldorf schools — the Waldorf school curriculum comprises 12 years, in many cases preceded by pre-school kindergarten where the emphasis is on imitation and imaginative play. As in some Scandinavian countries, but unlike many other Western countries, Waldorf education delays the start of formal learning until age six–seven, seeing the *change of teeth as critical for this.

Waldorf pedagogy holds that, in growing up, every human being passes through various developmental stages that parallel evolutionary stages of *humankind (see: Biogenetic law). For this reason, the teaching material in all classes takes each developmental stage into account. In Class Five, for instance, attention focuses on the era of Ancient Greece, since pupils at that age (11/12) are passing through a closely related developmental period in which body and spirit are harmoniously balanced, and physical prowess — for instance in the original form of the Olympic

Waldorf schools

Games — is at the same time matched by *beauty* of movement and inner stance.

Waldorf teachers seek to nurture and unlock the qualities and talents that each individual pupil bears within him, believing that every child brings particular qualities from before birth. To achieve this aim, equal attention is paid to the balanced development of *will, *feeling and *thinking, and teaching material is devised less from an intellectual or academic perspective than in order to fully address the child's whole being and changing developmental needs. Very generally, one can say that early years' education nurtures primarily the will, the middle school years speak to the child's developing feelings and aesthetic sense, and the upper school years address the young person's sense of truth in thinking and in formulating personal ideals. After completing the 12-year curriculum at a Waldorf school, students frequently go on to mainstream university and into every kind of profession.

Rudolf Steiner: *Study of Man*, GA 293; *Practical Advice to Teachers*, GA 294; *Discussions with Teachers*, GA 295; Francis Edmunds: *Introduction to Steiner Education: The Waldorf School*.

Warmth, sense of — one of the 12 *senses. It enables us to know both the actual temperature of our surroundings and also the warmth of soul that other people emanate. People who radiate enthusiasm provide their surroundings with warmth in every respect. The *'I' can engage fully in the body and its surroundings only when sufficient psychological and physical warmth is present. That is why it is important, especially for children, to be dressed warmly enough. Continual loss of warmth through scanty clothing depletes both physical and psychological resources and life forces. Red cheeks not only reveal physical warmth but also life-giving enthusiasm. The relationship between warmth and the 'I' also appears in blushing, when we see how a sense of embarrassment or shame works directly through the 'I' into the circulation of the blood and physical processes.

Rudolf Steiner: *Study of Man*, GA 293; Albert Soesman: *Our Twelve Senses.*

Wegman, Ita (1876–1943) — physician of Dutch origin; Rudolf *Steiner's closest colleague from 1922; founder of the first anthroposophical hospital in Arlesheim, Switzerland, now known as the Ita Wegman Clinic. She was the leader of the Medical Section of the School of *Spiritual Science in *Dornach, Switzerland, and co-wrote a fundamental work on medicine with Steiner (*Fundamentals of Therapy*). She was also responsible for developing a distinctive form of rhythmic massage, derived from Swedish massage, and for devising a range of external therapeutic applications using compresses and poultices.

J.E. Zeylmans van Emmichoven: *Who was Ita Wegman?*

Whitsun — or Pentecost. The Christian festival commemorating the descent of the Holy *Spirit, celebrated on the seventh Sunday after *Easter. Spiritual fire from heaven individualized itself in the shape of 12 flames on the heads of the 12 apostles, as described in Acts 2: 1–47. The third aspect of Holy *Trinity, the Holy *Spirit, here became manifest and has remained connected with *humankind ever since. This *festival heralds individualized and independent connection with the spiritual world, and emphasizes the power of human utterance to speak spiritual truths that all can understand, irrespective of differences of language and outlook. Real inspiration from the higher *'I' can guide us in life, rather than *instincts from the *physical body, habitual *urges from the *ether body, or *desires from the *astral body.

Rudolf Steiner: *The Reappearance of Christ in the Etheric*, GA 118.

Will — in the threefold division of *thinking, *feeling and

Will

will, the will is embodied in the metabolic system and limbs. The processes at this pole occur largely at an unconscious level, except where some disorder brings them to our awareness as pain. Neither are we aware of how our aims and intentions actually affect our physical processes so that, for example, our feet carry us to where we wish to go. The will is also characterized as 'a sea of *spirit' — the domain of the first *hierarchy. From this 'sea of spirit' a multitude of unconscious or subconscious impulses arise which originate in our personal *karma. In other words, we may 'find ourselves' in life situations which our ego, or lower *'I', is very dissatisfied with, but which have their higher purpose as learning experience, determined by the higher 'I'.

When growing up, the child experiences a metamorphosis of will impulses that gradually change into thinking processes (see: Waldorf schools). As the child learns increasing physical adroitness and mastery, the forces of growth and development that enabled him to do this are freed and can be employed in *thinking processes. Thinking is the metamorphosis of the will.

When we relate will impulses to the four human *members or bodily sheaths, increasing levels of conscious awareness give the following sequence: at the physical level will appears as *instinct*; at the level of the *etheric body it appears as *urge*; at the level of the *astral body, it appears as *desire*; and at the level of the *'I' the will appears as *wish, motivation and ideal*. When we know which member a certain will impulse originates from, we are better placed to evaluate and regulate it. In this sense, a 'hygiene of the will' can offer us insight into the mysteries of our own karma. 'Why do I want this situation/event?' is a question that can develop awareness of our deeper and otherwise unconscious will.

Rudolf Steiner: *Study of Man*, GA 293.

Wish — also called: motive, originating from the *'I'. See also: *will.

World ether — the *ether body of the *earth. Planet earth is enveloped in and penetrated by an ether body of its own, which sustains all living processes, along with currents in the oceans and atmosphere. Thus the earth is also a living organism.

Rudolf Steiner: *Mystery of the Universe*, GA 201.

World-word — also called: Word or Logos, referring to *God, as mentioned at the beginning of the Gospel of St John. The idea that the whole of Creation received its form through sound or utterance is one that can be traced back to Pythagoras, who speaks of the *Harmony of the Spheres. Research by Ernst *Chladni, and more recently by Alexander Lauterwasser and Masaru Emoto, also reveal this formative power of sound. The physical world can be regarded as a modification of spiritual concepts given shape by God's spoken Word.

Rudolf Steiner: *Harmony of the Creative Word*, GA 230.

Z

Zarathustra — Persian: 'gold star'. Greek/Latin: Zoroaster. Initiator of the Ancient Persian *cultural period (5067–2907 BC). Zarathustra was inspired by the sun god *Ahura Mazda. Exact dates of Zarathustra's life cannot be given since the name appears to be a universal nomenclature for a trend or group of initiates, rather than a personal name. Zarathustra drew the attention of people who were still largely *clairvoyant to the *earth. He taught them how to till the soil, develop grain from wild grasses, grow fruit from wild plants, and domesticate wild animals. Therefore, we clearly have here the beginnings of agriculture. One of his symbols is a gold dagger with which he opened up the earth, symbolic of agricultural activity.

D.J. van Bemmelen: *Zarathustra, the First Prophet of Christ*; Rudolf Steiner: *The Gospel of St Matthew*, GA 123.

Zodiac — arrangement of the stars in 12 sections or signs that from time immemorial were considered to be the language of the gods in the sky. This divine language is also found in the 12 figures of our clock, in the 12 disciples of *Jesus, and in ancient folklore in which the number 12 often plays an important role. The divine beings of the zodiac, also called *hierarchies, not only played a role in the creation of *mankind in a distant past, but still play an important part in the conception of a new baby. Thus the broadest conceivable circumference, the zodiac, influences the smallest conceivable element of life: the germ cell. In the extensive anthroposophical account of the hierarchies, the zodiac signs are depicted as living spiritual forces mirrored in all aspects of life on earth. Modern research has discovered the influences of planets and constellations on nature, for instance in the changing shape of plant buds during winter (Lawrence Edwards) or on the growth of vegetables and plants (Maria Thun). See: Biodynamic.

Rudolf Steiner: *The Spiritual Hierarchies and the Physical World*, GA 110.

Bibliography

By Rudolf Steiner:

The works of Rudolf Steiner are listed with the volume numbers of the complete works in German — the 'GA', or *Gesamtausgabe* — as published by Rudolf Steiner Verlag, Dornach. Titles given in English refer to the latest published editions. Where in print, these are available via Rudolf Steiner Press, UK (www.rudolfsteinerpress.com) or SteinerBooks, USA (www.steinerbooks.org).

GA 4   *The Philosophy of Freedom*. Also published as: *Intuitive Thinking as a Spiritual Path*

GA 7   *Mystics After Modernism*

GA 9   *Theosophy*

GA 10   *Knowledge of the Higher Worlds*. Also published as: *How to Know Higher Worlds*

GA 11   *Cosmic Memory*

GA 12   *The Stages of Higher Knowledge*

GA 13   *Occult Science, An Outline*. Also published as: *An Outline of Esoteric Science*

GA 14   *Four Mystery Dramas*

GA 16/17 *A Way of Self-Knowledge and The Threshold of the Spiritual World*

GA 23   *Toward Social Renewal*

GA 26   *Anthroposophical Leading Thoughts*

GA 27   *Extending Practical Medicine*

GA 28   *Autobiography*

GA 34   *The Education of the Child*

GA 40   Includes: *The Calendar of the Soul*

GA 57   Includes: *The Four Temperaments*

GA 58   Includes: *From Buddha to Christ*

GA 62   Includes: *The Poetry and the Meaning of Fairy Tales*

GA 67   Some material in: *Sleep and Dreams*

GA 83   *The Tension Between East and West*

GA 93a *Foundations of Esotericism*

GA 205	*Therapeutic Insights*
GA 210	*Old and New Methods of Initiation*
GA 217	*Becoming the Archangel Michael's Companions*
GA 223	Some material in: *The Cycle of the Year*
GA 230	*Harmony of the Creative Word*
GA 232	*Mystery Centres*
GA 233	*World History in the Light of Anthroposophy*
GA 234	*Anthroposophy and the Inner Life*
GA 236	*Karmic Relationships Vol. 2*
GA 240	*Karmic Relationships Vol. 6*
GA 243	*True and False Paths in Spiritual Investigation*
GA 245	*Guidance in Esoteric Training*
GA 260	*The Christmas Conference*
GA 266	*Esoteric Lessons 1904–19*
GA 279	*Eurythmy as Visible Speech*
GA 280	*Creative Speech*
GA 286	*Architecture as a Synthesis of the Arts*
GA 291	Some material in: *Colour*
GA 293	*The Study of Man*
GA 294	*Practical Advice to Teachers*
GA 295	*Discussions with Teachers*
GA 301	*The Renewal of Education*
GA 305	*The Spiritual Ground of Education*
GA 312	*Introducing Anthroposophical Medicine*
GA 313	*Anthroposophical Spiritual Science and Medical Therapy*
GA 315	*Eurythmy Therapy*
GA 317	*Education for Special Needs*
GA 319	*The Healing Process*
GA 322	*The Boundaries of Natural Science*
GA 327	*Agriculture Course*
GA 340	*World Economy*
GA 348	*From Comets to Cocaine*
GA 352	*From Elephants to Einstein*

Additional works (all various GAs):

Architecture, An Introductory Reader
The Festivals and their Meaning

'Meditations' series: *Breathing the Spirit | Finding the Greater Self | The Heart of Peace | Living With the Dead*
Mysteries of the Holy Grail
Strengthening the Will
Six Steps in Self-Development
Verses and Meditations

Other authors:

Bemmelen, D.J. van: *Zarathustra, The First Prophet of Christ*, Vrij Geestesleven 1968

Benson, J.L.: *The Inner nature of Colour*, SteinerBooks 2004

Blattmann, Georg: *The Sun, the Ancient Mysteries and a New Physics,* Anthroposophic Press 1985

Capel, Evelyn and Ravetz, Tom: *Seven Sacraments in the Christian Community*, Floris Books 1999

Childs, Gilbert: *Steiner Education in Theory and Practice*, Floris Books 1991

Dijk, Danielle van: *Christ Consciousness*, Temple Lodge Publishing 2010

Edmunds, Francis: *Introduction to Steiner Education: The Waldorf School*, Sophia Books 2004

Edwards, Lawrence: *The Vortex of Life*, Floris Books 1993

Emoto, Masaru: *The Hidden Messages in Water*, Beyond Words Publishing 2004

Goethe, J.W. von: *The Green Snake and the Beautiful Lily*, SteinerBooks 2006

Goudoever, H.D. van: *A Contemplation about Rudolf Steiner's Calendar of the Soul*, Rudolf Steiner College Press 1975

Grosse, Rudolf: *The Christmas Foundation; Beginning of a New Cosmic Age*, Steiner Book Centre 1984

Heidenreich, Alfred: *The Risen Christ and the Etheric Christ*, Rudolf Steiner Press 1969

Houten, Coenraad van: *Awakening the Will*, Temple Lodge Publishing 1999

Husemann/Wolff: *The Anthroposophical Approach to Medicine*, Anthroposophic Press 1996

Jacobs, Valerie: *Black and White Shaded Drawing*, Rudolf Steiner Press 1975

Jarman, Heather: *Mother Earth's Children*, Wynstones Press 1995
Judith, Anodea: *Eastern body, Western Mind*, Celestia Arts Publishing 1996
Jünemann, Margrit: *Painting and Drawing in the Waldorf School*, Hawthorn Press 1994
Kiersch, Johannes: *A History of the School of Spiritual Science, The First Class*, Temple Lodge Publishing 2006
Kirchner, Hermann: *Dynamic Drawing, Its Therapeutic Aspect*, Mercury Press
König, Karl: *Becoming Human: A Social Task*, Floris Books 2011
Lauterwasser, Alexander: *Water Sound Images, the Creative Music of the Universe*, Macromedia Publishing 2002
Lievegoed, B.C.: *Mystery Streams in Europe and the New Mysteries*, Anthroposophic Press 1982
Lehrs, Ernst: *Man or Matter*, Rudolf Steiner Press, 1985
Lommel, Pim van: *Endless Consciousness*, HarperCollins 2010
Lovelock, James: *Gaia: A New Look at Life on Earth*, Oxford University Press 1979
McAllen, Audrey: *Sleep*, Hawthorn Press 1981
Marti, Ernst: *The Four Ethers*, Schaumburg Publications 1984
Mees, L.F.M. MD: *Secrets of the Skeleton*, Anthroposophic Press 2005
Meyer, Rudolf: *The Wisdom of Fairy Tales*, Floris Books 1995
Olfers, Sibylle von: *The Story of the Root Children*, Floris Books, 1996
Oort, Henk van: *Anthroposophy, A Concise Introduction to Rudolf Steiner's Spiritual Philosophy*, Temple Lodge Publishing 2008
Opie, Iona and Peter: *Children's Games in Street and Playground*, Oxford University Press 1969
Poppelbaum, Hermann: *Man and Animal, Their Essential Difference*, Anthroposophic Press 1931
Prokofieff, Sergei O: *Relating to Rudolf Steiner*, Temple Lodge Publishing 2008
—*The Occult Significance of Forgiveness*, Temple Lodge Publishing 2004
—*Rudolf Steiner and the Founding of the New Mysteries*, Temple Lodge Publishing 1994
Querido, René M: *The Golden Age of Chartres*, Floris Books 1987

Selg, Peter: *Unbornness, Human Pre-Existence and the Journey towards Birth*, Anthroposophic Press 2010
Siegel, Daniel: *Mindsight*, Oneworld Publications 2010
Smit, Jörgen: *Meditation, Guiding Our Lives for the Encounter with Christ*, Rudolf Steiner Press 2007
Soesman, Albert: *Our Twelve Senses*, Hawthorn Press 1999
Stein, Walter Johannes: *The Ninth Century and the Holy Grail*, Temple Lodge Publishing 2009
Stibbe, Max: *Seven Soul Types*, Hawthorn Press 1992
Wilkinson, Roy: *Interpretation of Fairy Tales*, Rudolf Steiner College Press
Yates, Frances A.: *The Rosicrucian Enlightenment*, Routledge 1972
Zajonc, Arthur: *Catching the Light, the Entwined History of Light and Mind*, Oxford University Press 1993
Zeylmans van Emmichoven, J.E.: *Who was Ita Wegman* (three vols.), Mercury Press 1995-2005